John Wayne

A Tribute

John Wayne

A Tribute

Foreword by James Stewart

by Norm Goldstein | The Associated Press

Holt, Rinehart and Winston

New York

HRW BOOKS

The Associated Press would like to thank the following companies that produced and distributed the films of John Wayne: Columbia Pictures, Metro-Goldwyn-Mayer, Monogram Pictures, National General, Paramount Pictures, Republic Pictures, RKO Radio Pictures, 20th Century-Fox, United Artists, Universal Pictures, and Warner Bros.

Grateful acknowledgment is made for permission to reproduce photographs as follows: Museum of Modern Art/Film Stills Archive, p. 30; Penguin Photo, pp. 21, 23; Mark Ricci (Memory Shop, Inc.), p. 31.

Project Director: Dan Perkes
Author: Norm Goldstein
Photo Editor: Suzanne Vlamis
Photo Printer: Joe Greico

Designed by Allan Mogel

Published simultaneously in Canada by Holt, Rinehart and Winston of Canada, Limited.
Library of Congress Cataloging in Publication Data

Goldstein, Norm.
  John Wayne: a tribute.

   1. Wayne, John   2. Moving-picture
actors and actresses—United States—Biography.
PN2287.W454G6   791.43′028′0924-[B]   79-10811
ISBN 0-03-046781-0 Paperback
ISBN 0-03-053021-0 Hardbound

Printed in the United States of America
10 9 8 7 6 5 4

Contents

Foreword by James Stewart

John Wayne was probably the biggest star in the world . . . yet he retained the qualities of a small boy. He had the enthusiasm for life that would make a high school football star envious.

And through it all, Duke never changed. As a man he was exactly the boy he started out. And as a friend . . . well, you just wouldn't want a better one.

In his lifetime, Duke stamped AMERICA across the face of the motion picture industry. Few other men, living or dead, have ever portrayed the fine, decent, and generous American qualities as Duke did.

He portrayed on screen the values he lived off screen. Gentle. . . so much so, it would have surprised his critics. Loyal . . . once your friend, always your friend. Courageous . . . if you doubt it, remember his fight against cancer, or the way he faced heart surgery. And decent. Above all, Duke was a decent man.

He was also far from perfect. He made his mistakes as I have made mine and you have made yours. All in all, I would say they were unintentional. Mistakes of the heart, I would say.

Of course the man had faults . . . but I wouldn't be the one to cast the first stone.

Let me say this about the John Wayne I knew. He was an Original. He was the Statue of his Times.

All in all, I think it was the man's integrity that speaks most of him. His principles never varied. Nor did his ideals. Nor did his faith in mankind.

Jimmy Stewart

1

John Wayne leads the wagon train over the old Oregon trail in The Big Trail *(Fox, 1930).*

1
Beginning of the Trail

The nation was slipping into the Great Depression, but there was one young industry that would continue to prosper by taking America's mind off its troubles. The film industry had just taken a giant step forward: The movies emerged from their age of silence and had begun to talk.

In that year of 1930, Douglas Fairbanks Sr., Greta Garbo, and Tom Mix were the country's screen favorites. In that year, too, a train of events at Fox studios laid the foundation for another career that would rival—and far outlast—theirs.

Fox had just scored a success with the "first outdoor sound feature"—*In Old Arizona*—and planned to follow it with an ambitious Western called *The Big Trail,* the story of a pioneer trek along the Oregon trail.

As most studios did after the advent of sound, Fox raided the Broadway stage for the more mellifluous actors, and signed Marguerite Churchill for *Trail*'s female lead, along with Tully Marshall and Tyrone Power Sr.

Veteran director Raoul Walsh was still looking for the male lead to play the frontier scout when he noticed a tall young man carrying a chair into the property warehouse on the Fox lot. He had broad shoulders to go with impressive height, Walsh remembered many years later, and something else:

"Dammit, he looked like a man. To be a cowboy star you've got to be six-foot-three or over; you've got to have no hips and a face that looks right under a sombrero."

Walsh saw those things in the young man unloading a truck, juggling a "solid Louis Quinze sofa as though it were made of feathers," picking up a chair with his free hand. About six-four, 220 pounds, Walsh figured. When the young fellow came out for another load, Walsh went over and asked his name.

"The name's Morrison." He added he'd just come out of the University of Southern California and was working as a prop man, mostly on John Ford films.

The director liked the sound of his voice, the way he carried himself—big, but moving easily.

"What else can you do besides handle props?"

A slow grin. "I can play football."

"Let your hair grow," Walsh told him, "and come and see me in two weeks."

Two weeks later Morrison appeared, hair longer, wearing a buckskin outfit issued him by Fox wardrobe. He was tested by Walsh and Winfield Sheehan, the studio head.

"He'll do," Sheehan grunted afterward. "What did you say his name was?"

"Morrison."

"Sounds like a circuit preacher."

Walsh and Sheehan started scribbling names on

A snow-covered Wayne in his first leading role in The Big Trail.

paper. Walsh remembered the names of American pioneers and came up with one he'd always liked. He showed it to Sheehan.

"That's it," Sheehan said. "Wayne. Not Mad Anthony. Just John. John Wayne."

Walsh had his leading man. Morrison had a new name.

John Wayne, prop man and bit player turned actor, made no big splash—hardly a ripple—in that 1930 film, his first featured role. In retrospect, it was an inauspicious start to an incomparable career that was to span five decades and more than 150 films.

John Wayne. The name seems synonymous with American movies themselves. It's not a movie "with John Wayne," or even "starring John Wayne." It is, simply, "a John Wayne movie." The image is immediate and clear: rough and gruff; big and brawling; a strong American hero against the frontier, against the elements, against the enemy—and Good triumphant in the end.

John Wayne was one of a handful of movie greats whose popularity held up over the years despite an occasional run of bad films, and despite personal difficulties, marital and physical.

He was America's No. 1 box office lure in 1950 for the first of several times, and twenty years later he accepted his first Oscar as Best Actor. His films have earned more than half-a-billion dollars; at last count, seventeen of the one hundred biggest box-office attractions are "John Wayne movies."

In each and every year between 1928 and 1976—a lung cancer operation notwithstanding—at least one new John Wayne movie and sometimes half a dozen or more were released.

John Wayne always was larger than life, on screen and off, in Westerns and wars, in real controversy or reel conflict. He was indeed something of a Mt. Rushmore, in face and fame: solid and reliable, the perennial patriarch, personally and professionally symbolic to his admirers of old, simple, immutable American values.

John Wayne's trail began, appropriately, in America's heartland: Winterset, Iowa, about fifty miles southwest of Des Moines. Winterset was a town of three thousand on May 26, 1907, when Clyde "Doc" Morrison and his wife, the former Mary Brown, announced the birth of their first child. They named him Marion Michael.

The Morrisons were of English, Irish, and Scottish ancestry and Doc made his living as a druggist. Another son, Robert, was born five years later. Soon afterward, Doc came down with tuberculosis and was advised to move to a warmer climate.

Doc chose California. He homesteaded in true pioneer fashion on eighty acres of land on the edge of the Mojave desert near Lancaster. The family soon joined him there—"in a shanty," as Wayne remembers it. Here young Marion learned to ride and shoot (mostly rabbits and snakes).

Doc gave farming a valiant try but couldn't make a go of it. So the family moved seventy miles to Glendale, a Los Angeles suburb, where Doc resumed his occupation as a druggist and his eldest son helped out jerking sodas and running deliveries.

When Wayne was about nine, he got the nickname "Duke," which stayed with him even after he made his screen name famous. The origin was humble.

"I had a dog named Duke," as Wayne recalled. "Every fireman in Glendale knew that dog. They didn't know my name, but they knew the dog's. Next thing, they were calling me 'Duke,' too. I wasn't named for royalty; I was named for a dog."

Duke Morrison was a shy, awkward, introspective boy at the Doran Elementary School and at the Glendale Intermediate Junior High.

He adjusted and matured in Glendale High School, however, and became one of the most popular boys there. He was class president in 1925, worked on the school newspaper, the *Glendale Explosion,* headed various class committees—and was an A student. All this while he worked at odd jobs and played guard on an undefeated Glendale High football team; he was named to the All-Southern California eleven.

The combination of honor grades and all-star football got him a scholarship to the University of Southern California, though he would have preferred the United States Naval Academy at Annapolis. He had continued success in his first year at USC, joining the Sigma Chi fraternity and playing well on one of the better football teams in Trojan history.

The Trojans were quite an attraction in those pre-television days (as they still are) and tickets were hard to come by. Cowboy star Tom Mix, who had set up movie shop nearby, made a deal with the USC coach, Howard Jones. Mix got choice seats to the games and promised summer jobs to the football players in return.

Young Morrison needed work. His father wasn't doing well either at the drugstore or with an ice cream company he had tried.

"The Depression had started," Wayne recalled "and he simply was not a good businessman— although a fine man and a wonderful father."

Duke reported to the Fox studios that summer of 1926, and again the following year. He never returned to USC after that.

"I was given a job with the 'swing gang,' a kind of utility work outfit. My wages were $35 a week. My job

John Wayne at the beginning of his career in Somewhere in Sonora *(Warner Bros., 1933).*

John Wayne stars with Claire Trevor in John Ford's epic film Stagecoach *(United Artists, 1939).*

Vera Ralston and John Wayne seated in an 1820 vintage carriage get final instructions for a scene in The Fighting Kentuckian, *filmed in 1949.*

In 1957 John Wayne rides a camel instead of his usual horse in the United Artists film Legend of the Lost.

was to lug furniture and props around and arrange them on the set," Wayne said.

The first picture he remembered working on was *Mother Machree,* a 1927 film about a devoted Irish mother and her son, directed by John Ford. Prop man Wayne also was an unbilled extra in the movie, but, more significantly, it gave him the chance to meet Ford, the man who was to have the greatest influence on his career, perhaps his life.

On the set of *Mother Machree,* Ford teased Wayne into a football stance and left him with his face in the dust as he outmaneuvered the big guy. (Ford was six-feet-one.) Wayne got even when they tried it again, leaving Ford looking up from the ground. Ford had a good laugh about it, had lunch with Duke—and thus began a teacher-tyro friendship that later blossomed into a long-lasting collaboration of talents resulting in some of America's finest films, especially Westerns.

"I could see," Ford said later, "that here was a boy who was working for something—not like most of the other guys, just hanging around to pick up a few bucks. Duke was ambitious and willing to work. Inside of a month or six weeks, we were fast friends, and I used to advise him and throw him a bit part now and then."

Ford remembers another early incident, as reported in Peter Bogdanovich's filmography of the director. It was on the set of *Four Sons,* in 1928:

John Wayne was the second or third assistant prop man on that film, and I remember we had one very dramatic scene in which the mother had just received notice that one of her sons had died, and she had to break down and cry.

It was autumn, the leaves were falling, the woman sitting on a bench in the foreground—a very beautiful scene. We did it two or three times and finally we were getting the perfect take, when suddenly in the background comes Wayne, sweeping the leaves up. After a moment, he stopped and looked up with horror. He saw the camera going, dropped the broom and started running for the gate. . . .

We were all laughing so much we couldn't work the rest of the day. It was so funny—beautiful scene and this big oaf comes in sweeping the leaves up. He still remembers it.

(Wayne remembered it differently, however, with Ford taking the business far less amiably.)

Another Wayne bit part was that of an Irish peasant boy in *Hangman's House,* in 1928. He was one of the excited spectators at the fence, cheering a steeplechase race.

When Ford directed *Salute,* released in 1929, he brought in the whole USC football team for the story of a gridiron rivalry between Army and Navy. One of the other members of the USC team was Ward Bond—

In the 1963 film McLintock! *Wayne takes a flying leap toward a startled Maureen O'Hara.*

which started another close and lasting friendship for Wayne.

"They [Bond and Wayne] were both perfectly natural," Ford recalled, "so when I needed a couple of fellows to speak some lines, I picked them out and they ended up with parts. Wayne used to work for me during the summertime—laborer, third or fourth propman; we all liked him—and then he'd go back to college. Probably that's why I chose him to play this part—I knew him so well."

Wayne then played a bit part in Ford's 1930 submarine story, *Men Without Women,* and did some gutsy stunt diving, too, for extra money.

Still, what Wayne did for Ford were bit parts, fleeting extras that would wind up on the cutting room floor as often as not. It was Raoul Walsh who gave Wayne his first big break, the lead in *The Big Trail* at $75 per week. And Wayne was taught some useful things—for example, a stunt man instructed him in the fine art of knife-throwing. But when a Shakespearean-bred actor was called in to teach Duke how to "speak," it worked less successfully; classical elocution wasn't Wayne's style, even then.

Walsh encouraged him to play his part "with a cool hand, like I think you'd do on a football field. Speak softly but with authority, and look whoever you're talking to right in the eye."

Ironically, Wayne almost didn't make *The Big Trail.* He was in bed for three weeks with dysentery and got up to work only when Walsh told him they couldn't wait any longer.

In his first scene Wayne was supposed to ride alongside the covered wagons as character actor Tully Marshall came by on a mule and offered him a slug from his jug. "That blankety-blank Tully Marshall," Wayne recalled. "It was full of the worst rot-gut I ever tasted, and I had to swallow it or ruin the scene. Ordinarily I wouldn't have minded so much. But my throat was so raw that the liquor almost killed me."

Director Walsh wrote about the film and his new star in his autobiography:

> He stepped down off his horse and gave me that lopsided grin which was to become one of his trademarks.
> "How did I do, Mr. Walsh?"
> He was confident in himself by this time and looked as if he knew the answer. . . .
> My new leading man had made a fine frontiersman. His acting was instinctive, so that he became whatever or whoever he was playing. Later, under the direction of John Ford, he joined the ranks of the movie immortals.
> There is a lot of pride in the knowledge that I discovered a winner.

In 1970 Wayne won his first Oscar.

John Wayne in a scene from the movie True Grit, *1969.*

America's No. 1 box office star in 1950.

ABOVE LEFT:
John Wayne at the Hampshire House in New York City, March, 1955, after learning he was voted King of the Movie House Box Offices in 1954.

ABOVE RIGHT:
John Wayne and his wife, Pilar, at the annual Academy Awards presentations in Santa Monica, California, April, 1961. Wayne's film The Alamo was one of five pictures nominated as best of the year.

LEFT:
Dean Martin presents the Cecil B. DeMille award to John Wayne at the 23rd annual Hollywood Foreign Press Association awards dinner in Hollywood, February 1, 1966.

John Wayne over the years, beginning at the left with a photo
of him during his freshman year at the University of Southern
California. In the center is a 1941 photo; right Wayne in 1974.

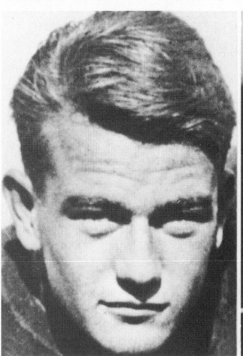

Wayne steps out of character to direct a scene in The Alamo.
He plays the role of Colonel David Crockett in the film.

Wayne appeared briefly in Salute, *which starred Frank Al-bertson and featured Ward Bond.*

Under the critical eye of director John Ford, James Stewart is slugging John Wayne during rehearsal for a scene from The Man Who Shot Liberty Valance (1962). *It was the first time Wayne and Stewart appeared together on the screen.*

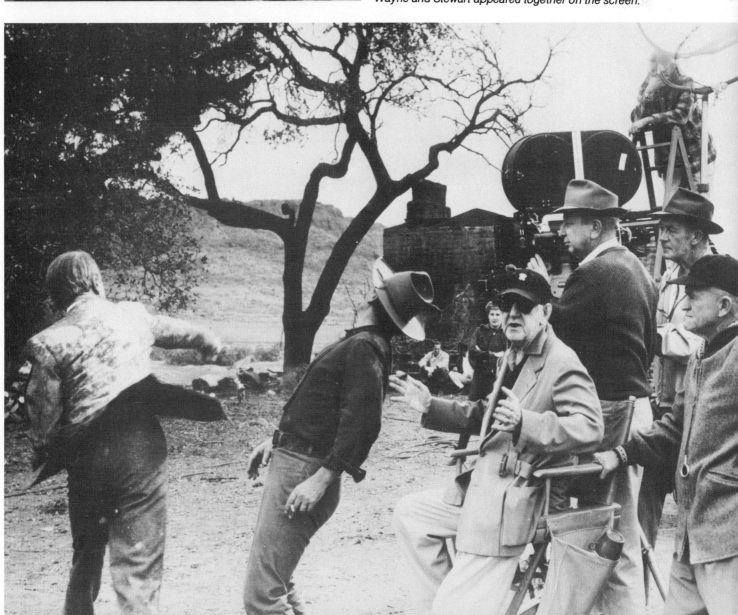

A very young John Wayne in uniform for Men Are Like That (Columbia, 1931).

Ward Bond (left) and John Wayne in one of their many screen collaborations The Long Voyage Home (United Artists, 1940).

Polly Ann Young with John Wayne in the Monogram Western The Man From Utah (1934).

Wagon train leader John Wayne with Marguerite Churchill, Helen Parrish, and David Rollins in The Big Trail.

John Wayne and David Rollins in The Big Trail *(Fox, 1930).*

2

John Wayne in The Lucky Texan, *one of the many Westerns he made for Monogram in the mid 1930s.*

2
Victory Deferred

Though Walsh had unquestionably discovered a winner, the victory would be deferred. *The Big Trail* itself was a box office flop, and didn't get Wayne off to a rousing start, even though he personally got good reviews. "Pleasingly natural," said one.

Much of *Big Trail*'s failure stemmed from the new wide-screen process in which it was filmed. In Depression time few theaters could afford to buy the equipment.

So Wayne got experience but little else from his first starring role, and he had a fistful of other troubles in those years.

His parents, holding on to a rocky marriage until John/Marion was college age and pretty much on his own feet, had finally separated and divorced. Wayne lost his football scholarship after an injury and didn't have enough money to return to USC following his sophomore year.

At the same time, he had fallen in love with Josephine Saenz, daughter of a Latin American diplomat, whom he met at a fraternity dance. Though she returned his feelings, her family objected to the marriage, and there was a clash of backgrounds; hers had been a strict Catholic upbringing.

Troubles with career, love, school, football—it all became too much, and Wayne sought a change of scenery by stowing away on a boat going to Hawaii. He

never made it off the boat. He came back to Fox.

There he wound up making a series of grade-B movies—most of them closer to Z—that are significant only for the further seasoning they gave him, and for the friends he made in those gloomy times.

It started with *Girls Demand Excitement,* a disaster about a rivalry between girls' and boys' basketball teams at a coed school. Wayne considered it probably the worst film in which he appeared.

Three Girls Lost wasn't much better, and was mildly described as "rather silly" in one review. It's interesting only in that it costarred Loretta Young. Also in the cast was Paul Fix, who was to become another Wayne friend and colleague over the years.

Harry Cohn, studio autocrat at Columbia Pictures then, signed Wayne to do *Men Are Like That,* with silent film star Laura LaPlante. The most flattering thing said about the stars was that they were "unconvincing." Wayne made a couple of other forgettable efforts for Columbia, but Duke—who worked for just about every major studio, some minor ones, and his own over the years—never again lent his name to a Cohn film. "King" Cohn's mistaken impression that Wayne was fooling around with one of his starlet-protégés ended that relationship for all time. Wayne made *Haunted Gold* for Warner Bros. before he fell into the serial rut with Mascot Pictures. That started

28

John Wayne in the 1931 film Girls Demand Excitement *(Fox).*

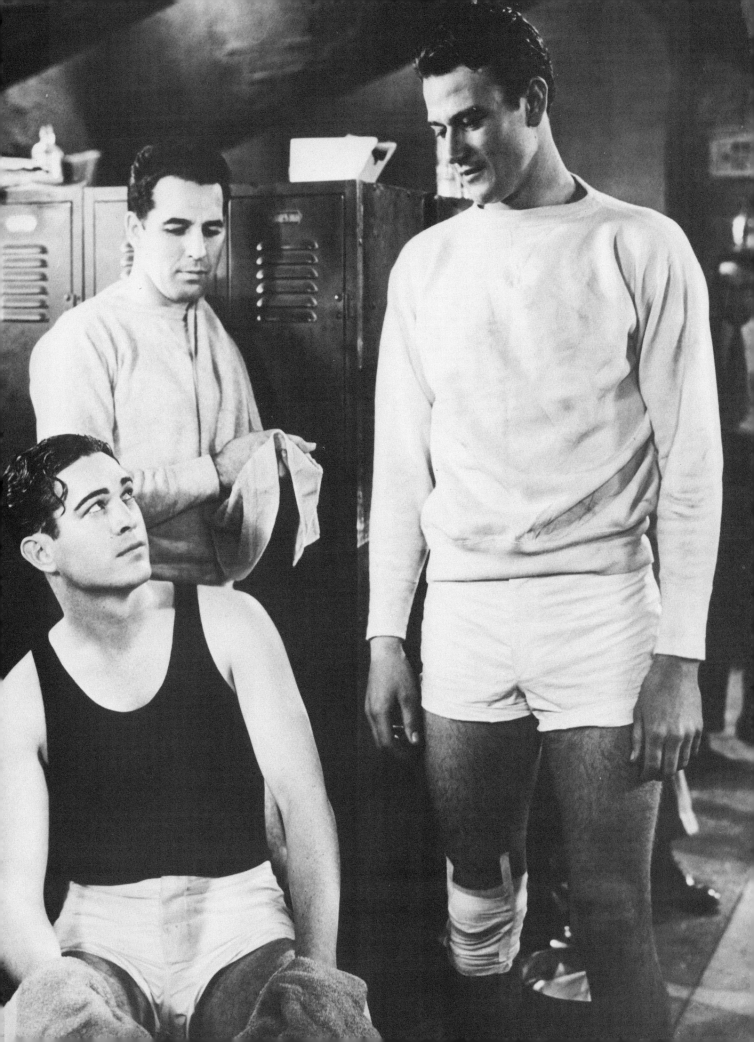

with *Shadow of the Eagle,* 12 two-reelers made quickly on what was appropriately known as Poverty Row. They were Charles Lindbergh-hero movies filled with aviator thrills and spills.

The Hurricane Express was another Mascot serial, with a railroad background.

The Three Musketeers was a serialized Foreign Legion version of the Dumas story.

Wayne worked at anything he could get. He was a prizefighter in *The Life of Jimmy Dolan,* a department store manager in *Baby Face* (with Barbara Stanwyck). He needed the money now, for he had at last, after a six-year courtship, married Josephine Saenz. Brother Bob was best man at the wedding in 1933 and Loretta Young, a friend of Josie's, a bridesmaid. The Waynes' first son, Michael, was born in 1934; Mary Antonia (Toni) two years later; Patrick in 1937; and Melinda in 1939.

Between 1933 and 1935 Wayne turned out no fewer than 16 five-reel Westerns for Monogram. None was memorable. The Wayne who, with the right direction and the right material, would ultimately raise some Westerns to a cinematic art form was scarcely visible on that Monogram treadmill.

In fact, he was shoved on a remarkably wrong track with the very first in the batch, a saga entitled

Wayne and his first wife, Josephine Saenz, in 1937 at a dinner in the Biltmore Bowl in Los Angeles.

Riders of Destiny and introducing "John Wayne as Singin' Sandy." It made him the first singing cowboy of the movies, before Gene Autry, Roy Rogers, and the others, and the miracle was that he didn't kill the idea forever. There's some dispute whether Wayne's gravelly voice was later dubbed, or merely naturally flat, but no matter; he sang for the sound cameras in what should be remembered as the first of the "hoarse operas." He had the wisdom to call a halt after a while.

"I played a character who always sang when he got mad," Wayne said. "Soon they started putting more and more songs into every picture. That was too much. I'm not a singer, so I quit." Gene Autry replaced him.

The Monogram avalanche and other movies that followed for Republic Pictures tagged Wayne as a B-grade Western actor. He himself referred to that period as the time of the "three-and-a-half-day Westerns."

Variety was not the spice of Wayne's acting life with those mass-produced saddle sagas, and even the titles echoed each other: Among the sixteen Wayne

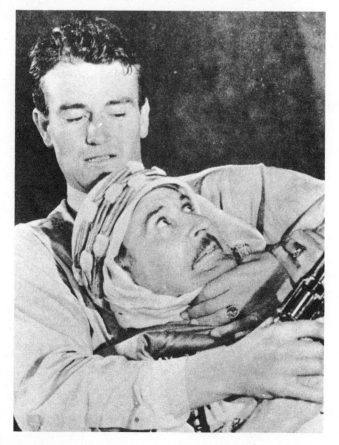

Wayne struggles with a sinister desert chieftain in The Three Musketeers *(Mascot, 1933).*

Loretta Young and John Wayne in a romantic scene from Three Girls Lost *(Fox, 1931).*

Max Terhune as Lullaby, William Farnum as Carson, John Wayne as Stony, Ray Corrigan as Tuscon, in Santa Fe Stampede, *a 1938 Republic picture.*

John Wayne with Earl Dwire and Jack Rockwell in the Monogram release The Lawless Frontier *(1934).*

Westerns released between 1935 and 1936 were *The Lawless Frontier, The Lawless Range,* and *The Lawless Nineties.* Probably no other actor mouthed the line, ''Saddle up; we'll head 'em off at the pass'' as often as Duke Wayne.

During those strenuous days he earned, and kept, his reputation as a hard-working, hard-drinking actor, though he rarely mixed the two. He saved the liquor for after the long day's shooting. Then, he would often go at it with fervor.

It wasn't until he contracted hepatitis after his 1978 heart surgery that he was banned from the bottle. He noted then:

''Sure I miss it. I could belt it pretty good—Bourbon, Scotch, Tequila—but I didn't go too far very often.''

Drinking was far from the only thing he learned in those early years of film-making. He learned his craft well, from coworkers he would never forget, on screen and off, in later years of success.

Once, in Ireland in 1951 filming *The Quiet Man,* Wayne asked about his longtime makeup man, Web Overlander. ''Where's the leprechaun?'' he inquired. He was told the producers had decided they didn't need him for that picture.

''Well, then,'' Wayne said, ''I've decided you don't need me either. When's the next plane home?''

Within the week, Overlander was on the set.

The closest of friends he was to make in those fledgling days, of course, was John Ford. The cantankerous Irish director constantly needled Wayne, from the very first prop man days. But Wayne worshipped him and no two professionals were ever closer.

Years later, Wayne beamed in displaying a makeup man's portrait of Ford hanging in his California home.

''Look how he captured that face I knew for fifty years; God, how I loved that man.''

Gene Autry, who broke into the B Westerns about the same time as Wayne, recounted a Ford-Wayne anecdote that is typical and telling of their relationship over the years.

It was during the filming of an NBC television special, *The Western,* at Autry's Melody Ranch, in 1958. Apparently, Wayne had been out partying the night before and arrived late on the set. Ford chewed him out like a headmaster berating a schoolboy.

''Duke just kept ducking his head and scuffing his toe in the sand and repeating, 'I'm sorry, boss.'''

But that didn't finish it. Ford ''punished'' him by demanding numerous run-throughs of a scene in which Wayne had to walk down a Western street, a

John Wayne and screen sweetheart Nan Grey in the 1936 Universal film The Sea Spoilers.

One of the rough and tumble moments for Wayne in the 1972 Warner Bros. film The Cowboys.

quarter-mile of red dust, under a blazing sun—"And you'll not get so much of a drop of water."

"Yes, boss," Wayne was said to reply.

But, later, Ford took Autry aside and told him to give Duke a healthy shot of Bourbon before they went on the air. And another shot halfway through the show—"but don't let him know that I know."

Autry complied. When Duke returned the empty bottle to him, he said, "Autry, you may have saved a man's life."

Years later Wayne sent Autry a photograph of himself as Rooster Cogburn, the character he played, with eyepatch, in *True Grit.* The inscription said: "Gene: A lot of water has run under the bridge. Whiskey, too."

In his biography, Autry commented: "Among the people I have enjoyed most on this wrinkled prune of a planet, Duke Wayne ranks near the top."

Among the other lifelong friendships cemented in Wayne's freshman film days were with Ward Bond (Wayne got him a role in *The Big Trail*),Grant Withers, and a part-Indian named Yakima Canutt. Wayne had worked with Canutt since his earliest days in film. Canutt taught him stunts, like falling off a horse without breaking his neck, and his riding manner. Wayne copied Canutt's drawl and his loping walk, and made them his own trademarks.

The two polished screen-fighting techniques, developing the near-miss swings that look so real when shot from an angle, and the use of table and chairs to smash over the villains' heads.

But Wayne was looking for a way out of B Westerns by now, and he got his chance from Trem Carr. Carr had brought Wayne into the Republic Westerns (Herbert Yates had merged several Poverty Row companies, including Monogram, into Republic) and he now was executive producer at Universal. Carr preferred Wayne in other roles, six between 1936 and 1937.

So Wayne appeared as a Coast Guard commander in *The Sea Spoilers;* a boxer in *Conflict,* with Jean Rogers and Ward Bond; a truck driver in *California Straight Ahead,* with Louise Latimer; a newsreel cameraman in *I Cover the War* ("get the picture—we don't screen alibis"); a hockey player in *Idol of the Crowds;* and a pearl diver who ships aboard a whaler in *Adventure's End.*

If Wayne had hoped for a turning point in his career, he was disappointed. All six pictures were flops, artistically and financially, and it was back to Republic and Herbert Yates—for less money. Now came a series of *Three Mesquiteers* pictures, Western takeoffs on the *Three Musketeers* theme. Wayne replaced Bob Livingston to round out a trio with Max

John Wayne and John Ford, seen here at Monument Valley, Utah, in 1971, remained close friends over the years.

John Wayne as Rooster Cogburn in the 1969 movie True Grit.

Terhune and Ray "Crash" Corrigan. (Mesquiteers is a play on the mesquite plant of the Southwest.)

By now Wayne had nearly a decade of low-grade, formula films. At thirty-one, he must have wondered if that was all the future would hold for him. Then John Ford called.

Montgomery Clift takes a picture punch from John Wayne in
Red River *(United Artists, 1948).*

Wayne is a lumberjack and prizefighter in Conflict *(Universal, 1936).*

Wayne gives costar Louise Latimer one of his famous grins in California Straight Ahead *(Universal, 1937).*

Wayne is a newsreel cameraman in I Cover the War *(Universal, 1937).*

Duke, seen here with Diana Gibson, plays a pearl trader and adventurer in Adventure's End *(Universal, 1937).*

3

Monument Valley provided a magnificent setting for Stagecoach.

3
Hitching a Stagecoach to a Star

John Ford's reputation was solidly established by 1937. The director had been at his trade since 1917, sometime writing and acting as well as directing, and he had brilliant successes both in silent and sound films, from *The Iron Horse* to *The Informer.*

Wayne and Ford had long since become fast friends, though always with a tinge of the mentor-pupil relationship, if not one of idol and worshipper. (Wayne also was the only person who could beat Ford at pitch, a variant of poker that Ford loved.)

So when the director summoned Wayne to his yacht that day in 1937, Duke expected nothing more fateful than another pleasant day of cards and booze with cronies Ward Bond, Grant Withers, and Victor McLaglen, the star of the masterful *The Informer.*

But Ford was alone. He wanted Wayne to read a screenplay, the story of a perilous journey through hostile Indian country in the Southwest. Would Wayne suggest somebody for the role of the Ringo Kid?

"Lloyd Nolan," Wayne proposed after he finished reading. Ford shook his head. The man he wanted, he said, was Duke Wayne. It was clear he'd had his old "third assistant prop man" in mind all along.

The director had chosen Wayne over the objections of producer Walter Wanger who was, understandably, unimpressed by Wayne's screen credits so far—mostly the run of low-budget, formula Westerns. But Ford stood firm.

Wayne was allowed to do many of his own stunts while shooting the picture, though the most dangerous ones were reserved for Canutt. At one point producer Wanger became alarmed. He saw Wayne atop a careening stagecoach firing at pursuing Indians and yelled, "Get that guy off there before he kills himself!" Duke was amused. "Hell, Wanger didn't know I'd been doing stunts like this for years just to eat," Duke said later.

The film, *Stagecoach,* with Claire Trevor, Andy Devine, Thomas Mitchell, Tim Holt, and Donald Meek, among others, was a critical and financial success when it was released through United Artists in 1939. For Ford it was another in a steadily lengthening list of superior films, perhaps his best Western. For Wayne it was a turning point in his career, which had threatened to stagnate among low-grade horse operas. And *Stagecoach* helped change the image of the genre itself.

Westerns had been a staple of the movie industry

42

Wayne's role in the 1939 United Artists production Stagecoach, *directed by John Ford, marked a turning point in his career.*

An interior scene from Stagecoach.

Marlene Dietrich plays chess with John Wayne during a break in the filming of Universal's Pittsburgh in 1942.

John Wayne, John Qualen, and Thomas Mitchell in The Long Voyage Home (United Artists, 1940).

A puzzled-looking Wayne holds his costar Jean Arthur in this scene from the 1943 film A Lady Takes A Chance.

since *The Great Train Robbery* in 1903, but through the silent era and long beyond, they were considered beneath critical notice (as many, indeed, were), simple and simple-minded entertainments for the small theaters of the hinterlands. The plots, it was pointed out, resembled each other like eggs, the action often seemed footage used over again from earlier shoot-'em-ups. The hero saved the widow's homestead and foiled the black-hearted villain. In the romantic Westerns of Tom Mix, Buck Jones, Hoot Gibson, and Ken Maynard, the hero wasn't even allowed to smoke or drink.

An upsurge in quality and quantity of Westerns in the 1930s, after the movies' adjustment to sound, hadn't done much to improve their reputation. They were still mostly B pictures, the lower half of the double feature, grist for the provinces and foreign countries.

Wayne, who became the colossus of the form—perhaps the "Last Cowboy"—always defended the Western, old style as well as new.

"Don't ever make the mistake of looking down your nose at Westerns," he said. "They're art—the good ones. Sure, they're simple, but simplicity is art.

"Westerns are terrific vehicles to tell a story. The horse is the best thing ever for showing motion. And Western landscapes make beautiful backgrounds.

"The Western is folklore and everyone understands it. My characterizations fit the legend, the folklore."

Stagecoach, at any rate, needed no apologies. It was visually beautiful, simple, and dramatically well-wrought. The acting of its talented cast under Ford's direction was notable. The film was literate, far from the drumfire clichés of run-of-the-mill Westerns. It was based on Ernest Haycox's short story, "The Stage to Lordsburg," and the screenplay was done by

Dudley Nichols, a favorite Ford writer.

Another star was born in *Stagecoach:* Monument Valley. A startling, stark expanse on the Utah-Arizona border, the location gave full play to Ford's sense of man's relationship to surrounding space, and Ford and Wayne were to use Monument Valley again and again.

Critical applause went mostly to Ford, the photography, and the stunts (Canutt and Wayne)—stunts that one reviewer described as having "the beauty of a ballet filled with danger."

Stagecoach was nominated for an Academy Award for Best Picture (only one Western, *Cimarron,* has ever received that Oscar, for 1930–31), but lost out to *Gone With The Wind* in a vintage year that also saw films like *The Wizard of Oz, Dark Victory, Wuthering Heights, Ninotchka, Of Mice and Men,* and *Mr. Smith Goes to Washington* on the ballot.

Thomas Mitchell did get a Best Supporting Actor award, and the film's composers and arrangers were recognized by the Academy. Ford got the Best Director's bow from the New York City Film Critics.

Stagecoach, in establishing a new standard for Westerns, accomplished even more for Duke Wayne. After his ten years as prop man, utility helper, bit player, featured actor, and "quickie" Western star, Wayne now graduated into A films, with a burst of new activity.

He worked hard, making about four or five films a year, most of them typically strenuous, some good, some bad. But when "Pappy" Ford called, Wayne would "drop everything and come running."

For Ford, he did *The Long Voyage Home,* based on several Eugene O'Neill one-act plays, in 1940. He reunited with Claire Trevor for *Allegheny Uprising,* and he worked once again with Raoul Walsh in *The Dark Command.* He teamed up with Paulette Goddard for a Cecil B. DeMille venture, *Reap the Wild Wind,* and he worked with Marlene Dietrich and Randolph Scott in both *The Spoilers* and *Pittsburgh.*

Meantime, World War II broke out and in 1941 Pearl Harbor involved the United States. Wayne tried to enlist as soon as war was declared. He was rejected because of age (Duke was thirty-four), family (four children), and a college football injury. Even Ford, then a lieutenant commander in the Navy and turning out fine documentaries, couldn't help.

Wayne did the next best thing. He often went overseas for the USO to entertain the troops. And in his movies he traded in his six-shooter for other kinds of guns in *Flying Tigers, Reunion In France, The Fighting Seabees, Back to Bataan* and, most notably, *They Were Expendable,* the last with Robert Montgomery.

In 1947 Wayne produced his first film, for Republic, *Angel and the Badman.* Critic James Agee noted: "John Wayne's first production mixes up Quakers with gun-bearing cowboys. The result is unpretentious, sweet-tempered, and quite likeable."

However, it was another Western, *Red River,* with

Wearing a ten-gallon hat, John Wayne entertains wounded American marines hospitalized in New Guinea in 1944.

(Left to right) John Wayne, Jesse Lasky, "Duckie" Louie, Ellen Drew, and Anthony Quinn on their way to Boston to take part in a benefit for wives of servicemen in 1945.

A U.S. Marine Corps colonel accepts a challenge from John Wayne during a visit to a 1944 movie set—and sends the star head over heels.

Duke, appearing in the film They Were Expendable, *signs autographs at a hotel party in Miami Beach, Florida, March, 1945.*

Wayne with Irene Rich on location in Sedona Valley, Arizona, for the film Angel and the Badman *(Republic, 1947).*

Montgomery Clift, that solidified Wayne's place at the top. He played an aging cattle baron in that film, a fine grim foil to the sensitive Clift. Because Wayne was only forty-one at the time, director Howard Hawks brought in character actor Walter Brennan to teach Wayne to walk like a tottery old man. Wayne would have none of it. "None of the outdoorsmen I knew were tottery," he said, and played it his way.

Wayne always had an instinctive sense of the ingredients that fit or didn't fit his formidable screen presence, and Howard Hawks was among those who admired it. "In making Westerns, I've worked practically just with John Wayne," he said; "he's by far the best."

Once when Hawks was trying to visualize a "pretty good Western story with somebody else in it" he conceded he was having trouble. "I know Wayne isn't suitable for it, but I'm going to miss his power and his force."

Red River, released in 1948, established Wayne's acting credentials. Bosley Crowther, movie critic for *The New York Times,* wrote:

> [Howard Hawks] has got several fine performances out of a solidly masculine cast, topped off by a withering job of acting a boss-wrangler done by Mr. Wayne. This consistently able portrayer of two-fisted, two-gunned outdoorsmen surpassed himself in this picture.

Sweet music to Duke's ears, though hardly more satisfying than John Ford's comment. Ford had never been shy with criticism of Wayne in his earlier quickie Westerns. After Ford saw *Red River,* he said: "I never knew the big fellow could act."

Ford put him in three pictures in the next two years, certainly among the best Westerns produced by the pair of talents. First was *Fort Apache,* a cavalry picture with Henry Fonda. Then, *Three Godfathers,* with Harry Carey Jr. and Pedro Armendariz. (The film, incidentally, a remake of Ford's silent movie, *Marked Men,* was dedicated to the star of the earlier one, Harry Carey Sr., who died the year before. Carey and his wife, Olive, were also close friends and advisers of Wayne's.)

The third Ford-Wayne picture in that period was *She Wore a Yellow Ribbon,* a rousing cavalry movie with Joanne Dru, John Agar, and Victor McLaglen, and filmed, again, in Monument Valley.

In 1949 Wayne played Sergeant John M. Stryker in *Sands of Iwo Jima*—and got his first Academy Award nomination for Best Actor. One reviewer found him "especially honest and convincing. . . . His performance holds the picture together." However, Broderick Crawford got the 1950 Academy vote for his role in *All The King's Men.*

John Wayne as Tom Dunson, with screen foster son Montgomery Clift and Walter Brennan, in Red River.

Wayne in a fight scene from Red River *(United Artists, 1948).*

Mae Marsh and Duke Wayne take a break during the filming of The Fighting Kentuckian.

Wayne relaxes with coactor Philip Dorn on the Hollywood set of The Fighting Kentuckian.

Duke Wayne was named No. 1 box office champion in the country for 1950, a feat he was to repeat the next year and often again. He was among the Top Ten longer and more often than any other movie favorite, the movies' most consistent drawing card.

He didn't let up his work schedule. He and Bob Fellows set up their own production company in 1951 (it later became Batjac Productions from a name in *Wake of the Red Witch),* for which Wayne did *Big Jim McLain, Island in the Sky, Hondo,* and *The High and the Mighty* (Spencer Tracy didn't want it) in the early 1950s. And he produced—but didn't appear in—*The Bullfighter and the Lady,* with Robert Stack.

And there were *The Wings of Eagles, The Searchers—*and the very special *The Quiet Man.* That classic, filmed in Ireland, earned director Ford an Academy Award and remained one of Wayne's favorites, along with *Stagecoach.*

The Quiet Man is about an ex-prizefighter who returns to his Irish roots and falls in love (with Maureen O'Hara). The picture is memorable, among other reasons, for the sprawling brawl across the rolling hills between Wayne and Victor McLaglen, who plays O'Hara's brother. It is surely among the best of the fight scenes, staples in Wayne films. Ironically, Wayne's rough-and-tough screen image—as well as his brawny build in reality—made him a target for many seeking to take on the fastest fists in the movies, whether out of pure daring or drunkenness.

Wayne always said he could hold his own in a fight, but he much preferred to avoid them.

''My usual way,'' he said, ''is to become deadly quiet, stretching to my full height. If this doesn't work, I have a use of the English language so filthy and insulting it scares them more than my fist.''

Once, however, in Sante Fe, New Mexico, a stranger in a bar waved around a bandaged hand and declared he had knocked Wayne cold. Wayne, peacefully asleep and unbattered, was awakened and told the story.

He dressed and went down to the bar in search of the story-telling stranger.

Wayne grabbed him by the collar and picked him up off the floor.

''Did you have a fight with me tonight?'' Wayne demanded.

The stranger stammered, ''N-n-no.''

Wayne held him up a few more seconds and dropped him. ''Okay,'' Duke said and stalked off.

Much of his off-screen brawling was not with strangers, but with his best friend, Ward Bond.

''Somehow an argument would start on the set,'' one cameraman recalled, ''and before long Ward and

Wayne talks with Rex Allen about Allen's first film, Arizona Cowboy, *on a studio lot in Hollywood, April, 1949.*

Duke would be going at it. They never stopped with a bloody nose or a black eye; they kept at it until they were both worn out.''

Bond and Wayne would often challenge each other in feats of strength at the Hollywood Athletic Club. Once, it got a little out of hand and the pair wrecked the club's locker room.

''Duke knocked Ward into a row of lockers, then Ward got up and knocked Duke down,'' remembered one witness. ''After that, we all got out and let them have the place to themselves until they were finished.''

The fighting duo paid a large bill for damages.

Aside from brawling and working together, Bond and Wayne often fished and hunted with each other.

Once, on a quail hunt, Wayne accidentally fired a charge of bird shot into Bond's back. Wayne took him to a hospital and later answered reporters' questions about the incident.

With a deadpan expression, Wayne told them: ''I'd never had a chance to check the pattern my gun makes. I was happy to see that the shot in Ward's back hadn't scattered at all.''

Duke and John Agar rest during a break in the filming of The Sands of Iwo Jima *on location at the Marine Corps' Camp Pendleton, near San Diego, July, 1949.*

John Wayne and Adele Mara (center) *line up with Herbert Yates, president of Republic Pictures* (next to Wayne), *Charles Skouras, head of Fox West Coast theaters* (far right), *and others, for the Hollywood premiere of* Sands of Iwo Jima, *January, 1950.*

Wayne accepts his Foreign Press Association award as the most popular actor of 1952 from actress Greer Garson. The presentation was made February 14, 1953, in Santa Monica, California.

As a birthday suprise, Barry White of Clapham, England, meets his American movie hero Duke Wayne at the Granada Cinema, Tooting, in London in 1951.

John Wayne, on location in Utah, portrays Lieutenant Colonel Kirby Yorke in the film Rio Grande. (Republic, 1950).

53

Wayne solidified his box office popularity in the 1950s, starring in twenty films in the decade. Many, interestingly, were not Westerns: *Blood Alley,* with Lauren Bacall, takes him through Chinese waters; in *Legend of the Lost,* with Sophia Loren, he's a Sahara Desert guide.

Three of his films in this period were for mystery man producer Howard Hughes: *Jet Pilot, Flying Leathernecks,* and *The Conqueror* (in which he's Genghis Khan).

In 1958 he made his first—and last—film for director John Huston, *The Barbarian and the Geisha.* The original title was *The Townsend Harris Story,* after the man who was American consul to Japan in the 1850s.

Axel Madsen's biography of John Huston quotes the director's reply to a question about casting the Harris role:

> Only one man is right for him and that's John Wayne. I want to send Duke's gigantic form into the exotic world that was the Japanese empire in the 1800s. Imagine! The massive figure, with his bluff innocence and naiveté, with his edges rough, moving among these minute people.
> Who better to symbolize the big, awkward United States of a hundred years ago? Duke's our man.

Those were probably the last kind words to pass between the two.

Wayne found the director slow, tedious, and obsessed with what Duke considered irrelevant detail. They never agreed on the approach to the film or Wayne's role in it.

"Huston had me walking through a series of Japanese pastels. Hell, my fans expect me to be tall in the saddle," Wayne complained.

One scene required setting fire to a Japanese village while Wayne is arrested by the Japanese governor. Huston called for a second take of the scene, while the fire continued to spread dangerously close to the principals. Then he shouted for yet another take and things were even hotter.

By the time the director yelled, "Cut!" Wayne had scorched his leg and an arm.

When shooting ended, Wayne and Huston weren't speaking to each other.

Jeff Hunter joins John Wayne in Warner Bros. 1956 film The Searchers, *with majestic Monument Valley as the backdrop for this John Ford film.*

John Wayne and four of his children on the Hollywood set where the young Waynes made their film debut in The Quiet Man *in 1951. Left to right are: Toni, Patrick, John, Melinda, and Michael.*

Wayne waves to fans at the London premiere of Rio Grande,
March 2, 1951.

John Wayne, Virginia Mayo, and Charles Coburn during pre-speech entertainment at a Dwight D. Eisenhower rally in Los Angeles, October, 1952.

LEFT:
In November, 1952, Joan Crawford presents John Wayne with a citation from The Interstate Circuit of Theatres for his community work and unselfish patriotism.

OPPOSITE:
John Wayne shows the two Oscars he accepted for Gary Cooper and John Ford to two former Academy Award winners, Olivia de Havilland (left) and Janet Gaynor (right) after the annual awards ceremony in Hollywood, March, 1953.

Associated Press writer Hal Boyle interviews John Wayne at New York's Hampshire House after he was voted King of the Movie Box Offices.

Wayne is hospitalized at Marin General Hospital, San Rafael, California, January, 1955. He strained his back during the filming of Blood Alley at nearby China Camp.

Actress Jane Wyman and John Wayne at a Hollywood gathering in May, 1953.

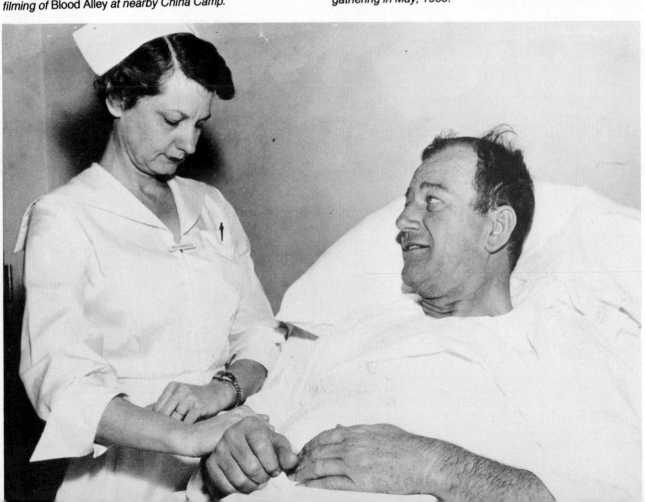

Sophia Loren and John Wayne jump over the iron parapet surrounding a fountain in the Piazza Navona during Wayne's visit to Rome in 1956 to prepare for Legend of the Lost.

Sophia Loren's punch jolts Wayne in a scene from Legend of the Lost.

Wayne appears amused as Loren demonstrates her shooting ability at a Rome shooting gallery.

Duke and Sophia Loren are joined by Tony Perkins on the set of Legend of the Lost *at Rome's Cinecitta, March, 1957. Perkins was working on another film at a nearby studio.*

Assisted by movie set workmen, Wayne bandages his right ankle which was dislocated when he fell during the shooting of *Legend of the Lost* in the Libyan desert.

Producer-director Dick Powell and John Wayne on location in St. George, Utah, July 30, 1954, for the movie *The Conqueror.*

Duke visits the Soviet Memorial near the Brandenburg Gate in Berlin, January, 1956. Wayne visited Berlin for the German premiere of The Conqueror.

Achtung!
Sie verlassen
nach 70m.
West-Berlin

YOU ARE NOW
LEAVING
BRITISH SECTOR

Japanese actresses surround John Wayne in the Tokyo
Airport VIP lounge where he arrived to film John Huston's
The Barbarian and the Geisha in 1957. (Left to right) Hiroko
Santani, Hitomi Nakahara, Utako Mitsuya, and Toyomi Karita.

*Wayne enjoys a break with his leading lady, Eiko Ando, on
the location site of* The Barbarian and the Geisha, *shot in
Kyoto, Japan, December, 1957.*

Wayne is surrounded by admirers outside a courtroom during the divorce proceedings.

4

4
Trouble Along the Way

Well before Wayne had reached the secure heights of his screen domination, his marriage with Josie, whom he had won with such patience and difficulty, had begun to fall apart.

Josie, with her strict Catholic upbringing of Spanish heritage, had different attitudes to life and family than did Duke. She shone as a society hostess. (The story, according to one of Duke's friends, was that Wayne was always sure of one priest home at dinner—he just wondered whether there would be two or three.)

Wayne, on the other hand, lived for his work, a couple or ten drinks at home after, and the camaraderie of his movie cronies.

Their paths separated legally in 1943, with an uncontested divorce the following year. Josie got a cash settlement, a percentage of Duke's earnings for life, and custody of the four children, for whom a trust fund was set up.

Later, he would acknowledge: "She's responsible, in breeding and behavior, for what they turned out to be. . . . Josephine never kept my kids from me."

By the time of their divorce Duke had met Esperanza Baur Diaz Ceballos—"Chata," for short, from the Spanish colloquial for "pugnose." He met the black-haired beauty, fourteen years his junior, in Mexico. She was a film actress and Wayne persuaded

Herbert Yates at Republic to put her under contract. She and Wayne were married in 1946.

Duke's mother, then Mrs. Sidney Preen, gave a wedding reception. (His father had died of a heart attack eight years earlier.) Ward Bond was best man.

It was a volatile marriage with Chata, the details of which flared up in ugly divorce proceedings in a California court in 1953. Court records of their stormy life in Encino, where Chata's mother had lived with them, told of charges and countercharges about who was unfaithful to whom (and if), who was the more violent when drunk, and who "clobbered" whom in shows of anger.

At one point in the trial, Duke's women fans held up a sign outside the courtroom: "John Wayne, You Can Clobber Me Any Time You Want."

In an unusual decision, the judge granted a divorce to each of the combatants. Chata returned to Mexico City. (She died there in 1954.)

It wasn't long before Wayne found wife No. 3: Pilar Palette, a diminutive Peruvian beauty. They were married in November, 1954, in Hawaii, where Duke was filming *The Sea Chase*.

A month after his third (and her second) marriage, Wayne told AP Hollywood reporter Bob Thomas that he had no special preference for Latin women; it was just coincidence that he had married three of them.

John Wayne and Esperanza Baur Diaz Ceballos apply for a marriage license in Los Angeles.

Wayne and his bride, Esperanza, step from a church after their marriage in a semiprivate ceremony in Long Beach, California, January 17, 1946.

71

Explained Wayne: "I've never been conscious of going for any particular type. They say a man follows a pattern, but I haven't been aware of it myself. Each of the women I married had been entirely different.

"I certainly don't have anything against American women. As a matter of fact, my wives have been as much American as they have been Latin. None of them speaks with an accent.

"My first wife had a French and Spanish mother and father, but she was brought up in Texas.

Esperanza spent a lot of time in this country and Pilar has been here a great deal and speaks English perfectly."

The marriage with Pilar produced three children: Aissa, John Ethan, and Marisa.

Aissa played the little girl in *The Alamo*; she was four when the picture was filmed. Indeed, *The Alamo* was a family affair for the Waynes and a long, long labor of love that was to prove one of the major disappointments of Duke's life.

John Wayne holds hands with his new bride, Peruvian actress Pilar Palette, during the outdoor ceremony at Kona, Hawaii, in November, 1954. (Left) John Farrow, who gave the bride away. (Right) District Magistrate Norman Olds, who performed the ceremony, and Mrs. Mary St. John and Francis Brown of Pebble Beach, California, the best man.

Wayne carries his bride, Pilar, from the plane on their arrival in New York City in January, 1955.

Duke prepares to take Pilar and their week-old daughter, Aissa, home from St. Joseph's hospital in Burbank, California, April 6, 1956.

John Wayne and his three-year-old son, John Ethan, on the Hollywood set of El Dorado, *January 11, 1966.*

The Waynes pose with their infant daughter, Marisa Carmela, at their home in Newport Beach, California, in early March, 1966.

Between scenes, Wayne congratulates his daughter Aissa, four, on her debut performance in the Texas epic The Alamo.

*Wayne and his wife, Pilar, sail to Europe on the French liner
Liberté, May 10, 1957.*

5

John Wayne as Davy Crockett in The Alamo.

5
Remember the Alamo?

John Wayne's home in Newport Beach, California, reflected his lifelong devotion to the Old West and its American folklore. He had paintings and sculptures by Western artists Frederick Remington and Charles Russell. He also had sizable collections of period guns, Hopi Indian kachina dolls, and photographs of Indians of the West. Wayne's fascination for that rough-and-tumble period of American history culminated in something very much like an obsession. He would film the story of that troop of 187 Texans who in 1836 fought valiantly but in vain against 3,000 Mexican soldiers in the battle of the Alamo.

Duke was determined to produce and direct the picture himself. He also wanted to play the part of Sam Houston, a figure that dominated his private pantheon. Wayne worked on the picture intermittently for nearly ten years; it took two years just to build the replica of the Alamo at Brackettsville, Texas. Almost every cent he had went into the picture. He got the rest he needed from wherever he could. He spared no expense.

The picture became something of a family affair with his young daughter, Aissa and his son Patrick acting in the film and his son Michael working as assistant to the producer. Duke wound up portraying Davy Crockett, with the role of Sam Houston going to Richard Boone.

His Batjac company spent an estimated $12 million—$50,000 just for the Hollywood premiere party—and the movie was nominated for Best Picture. Another sizable sum was spent on publicity in campaigning for the Oscar.

The Alamo was something Wayne felt he had to say, a personal statement that embodied the values for which he stood. Somehow, the brave American stand at the Alamo summed it all up for him. "This is the big American story that I didn't think anyone could do better than I. It's the first time in my life that I've been able to express what I feel about people."

But *The Alamo* won only one minor award, for Best Sound, and was generally panned by reviewers. The picture lost Wayne a fortune.

That year, 1960, brought Wayne other grief. Grant Withers, a friend of thirty years' standing, died. One year later Duke lost Beverly Barnett, likewise a close friend and his longtime press agent.

And then he lost Ward Bond. Wayne spoke the eulogy at the funeral of the man he played football with at USC, worked with in films over three decades, caroused and joked with—and whom he had loved dearly.

"We were the closest of friends, from school days right on through. This is the way Ward would have wanted it—to look out on the faces of good friends. He was a wonderful, generous, big-hearted man."

Visiting San Antonio, Texas, in 1960, Duke shakes hands with marines of the 14th Infantry Marine Corps reserve unit. They reenacted the march made by the men of Gonzales to the Alamo in 1836.

Wayne lines up a scene during the shooting of The Alamo.

John Wayne as director of The Alamo.

Bond used to joke about being known as "the fellow who's always in those John Wayne movies." Of course, he became a star in his own right when he took over as Major Seth Adams in the television series *Wagon Train.*

John Ford, who would tease Bond about appearing in the "phony TV Western," once directed an episode in the series—on condition he could bring along an actor he wanted to use and test for the movies. The actor was billed as "John Morrison." That episode with John Wayne was shown after Bond's death.

Dark days for Wayne, but, in reflecting on his life in 1960, he told a *Look* Magazine interviewer:

> I'm fifty-three years old and six-four. I've had three wives, five children, and three grandchildren. I love good whiskey. I still don't understand women, and I don't think there is any man alive who does.
>
> I've been around movies long enough for millions of people to have been born, had kids and died.
>
> But *I'm* still working.

And work he did. *North to Alaska, The Comancheros. The Man Who Shot Liberty Valance*—returning to the big, sprawling, brawling Westerns he knew so well. *Hatari!* (big game in Africa, sometimes referred to as his "veldt Western"). An episode in *The Longest Day.* A role in the Civil War sequence of *How The West Was Won. Donovan's Reef. McLintock!*—produced by Michael Wayne. A Roman centurion in *The Greatest Story Ever Told.* An Otto Preminger film, *In Harm's Way.*

He was tired, unusual for him. And lately he'd been bothered by pressure in his chest.

Pilar insisted that he go for a checkup.

Tennis star Althea Gibson is congratulated by Wayne and Holden on her selection as Female Athlete of the Year in an annual AP poll. She made her movie debut with the two actors in The Horse Soldiers *(United Artists, 1959).*

Duke chats with Maria Cooper, daughter of Gary Cooper, at a benefit party in Hollywood, May 14, 1960.

John Wayne and his wife, Pilar, arrive for the Academy Award presentations in Hollywood.

Time out for a chess game during the filming of The Comancheros *in 1961. Wayne is flanked by son Patrick* (left) *and Stuart Whitman on the Moab, Utah, set.*

John Wayne leaves from New York City for Paris in January, 1962, to film The Longest Day.

A few months after having lung surgery the Duke leaves Los Angeles for Durango, Mexico, to start filming The Sons of Katie Elder.

6

6

True Grit

John Wayne, a man who lived hard, drank hard, and smoked four packs of cigarettes a day, checked into Good Samaritan Hospital on September 16, 1964. A hospital representative discreetly said it was for the treatment of an old ankle injury.

After a few days it was announced that he was being treated for an "abscess in one lung." Surgery was performed and in due course Wayne was sent home. A newsman asked the fifty-seven-year-old actor whether he had cancer.

"I guess not," he replied.

In December he held a news conference to disclose that the hospital stay had been for removal of "cancer of the lung—and I have licked it."

Why hadn't it been announced right away?

"My advisers all thought it would destroy my image, but there's a lot of good image in John Wayne licking cancer—and that's what my doctors tell me."

He added: "I was lucky. I'd never been sick before in my life, but I always took an annual checkup at the Scripps Clinic in La Jolla. The X-rays showed a spot on my lung. They brought me to Los Angeles to Good Samaritan Hospital and opened me up. I was under intensive care treatment for more than a week while the doctors removed the malignancy.

"I thought, 'I was saved by early detection. Movie image or not, I think I should tell my story so that other people can be saved by getting annual checkups.'"

Pilar said that Duke "wanted to tell everybody right from the start; we never lied to anyone. When they asked us if he had heart trouble, we said no. And when they asked us if he had cancer, we also said no—because the doctors told us they got it all. Fortunately, no one asked if he had had cancer."

Later, when he was already back at work, Wayne elaborated on his encounter with a mortal threat: "It was like someone hit me across the gut with a ball bat. I stood shocked.

"Naturally, I thought about the possibility of death, but that isn't what bothered me the most. It was that feeling of helplessness. I just couldn't see myself lying in bed, not being able to help myself—no damn good to anybody. That, to me, was worse than the fear of dying.

"I was going to skip the checkup because I couldn't work it into my schedule. I thank the man upstairs for everything. He was looking after me.

"And my wife, Pilar, urged me to go to Scripps Clinic in La Jolla. They took pictures of me there and found something as big as a golf ball on my lung. They said, 'It's got to be cancer.' And they told me they wanted Dr. John Jones at Good Samaritan in Los Angeles to operate on me immediately. That urgency kind of shook me up.

Duke and his sons Patrick (left) and Michael confer before leaving Hollywood for location filming of McLintock! *in 1962 in Nogales, Arizona.*

John Wayne congratulates Adolph Zukor during Zukor's ninetieth birthday celebration in 1963.

Five-month-old John Ethan visits his dad during the filming of Donovan's Reef *on the Hawaiian island of Kauai, October 5, 1962.*

Muddied but cheerful, Wayne and Maureen O'Hara share a laugh during the filming of McLintock!

"Then came the job of breaking the news to my family. Pilar took it like a soldier—so did my two oldest boys, Michael and Patrick, although Patrick looked as if he were in a slight state of shock. And Toni and Melinda, my oldest daughters, they took it with tears. My young children, Aissa and John Ethan, were too little to tell, thank God. I thought a lot about them. Here they were, pretty young to be left without a father.

"I knew the four oldest kids could take care of themselves. They're grown up. But those little ones worried me.

"And my mother? How could I tell her? She wouldn't even see the last half of *The Alamo* because it was the first time I ever got killed on the screen. Thank God, I didn't have to tell her. She heard it from someone else in the family first.

"I had been hoping that maybe they could send that thing down my throat and burn the tumor off without cutting me. No chance. Jones said the thing was too big even to go in from the front, that he would have to go at it through the back. He said that way they could spot any tentacles that might have grown out from the tumor.

"So he cut me. He took half a lung—the lower half of my left lung. He also took a rib, moved my diaphragm up and my stomach over.

"When it was all over and I was able to be halfway my old self again, I wanted to tell everybody that I had cancer and was cured. But you know how it is in this business. Everybody is telling you that it would destory your image. I went along for a while until I got back on my feet and then I thought I owed it to people to tell the

Wayne talks with Loretta Young at the How the West Was Won *premiere.*

Duke, on vacation in 1963, strolls along the harbor of the Italian Riviera resort Santa Margherita Ligure where his yacht is docked.

Director Henry Hathaway gets a warm hello from Wayne at the airport in Madrid.

John and Pilar Wayne at the Hollywood premiere of How the West Was Won *in February, 1963.*

Henry Hathaway directs the first scene of the 1964 Circus World *in which Wayne stars with Lloyd Nolan (left) and Claudia Cardinale. Location for the scene is the Barcelona Opera House in Spain.*

advantage of early checkups. Maybe, to give hope to someone who had cancer.

"If I can help some poor devil—or at least give him hope—then I'm repaid enough."

Like other men who have walked through the valley of the shadow, Wayne eased back into normal life with a heightened appreciation for its blessings. "My family is more important to me than ever," he said. "Every day is precious to me now."

Early the next year he was in Durango, Mexico, filming *The Sons of Katie Elder,* which Duke described as a "ridin', jumpin', fightin' picture—a typical John Wayne Western, so you know I have to be in good health. I didn't get famous doing drawing room comedies."

Pilar and two of their youngsters had come down to the Mexican location with him. The work was difficult for a healthy man, much less a near fifty-eight-year-old with half a lung missing.

"It only hurts when I climb on a horse, which is something I do a lot of in my movies. It feels okay when I'm riding," said Wayne.

He felt fine generally, he insisted, though "I probably should have waited a little longer before starting this picture. It's a pretty rugged part. I love my business, but my pictures usually aren't on the easy side.

"I'm damn glad to be alive. And the doctors say I will be—barring accidents—for some time."

John Wayne was certainly alive. After *The Sons of Katie Elder,* he filmed two more Westerns: *The War Wagon,* with Kirk Douglas, and *El Dorado,* with Robert Mitchum. Then, *Cast a Giant Shadow.* He was even persuaded by Dean Martin to do a television guest shot.

Then, in 1966, in a belated answer to a Defense Department request for entertainers to tour the combat zones, John Wayne went to Vietnam.

90

Duke includes two Mexican chili peppers as part of his lunch during a break in the filming of the 1965 movie The Sons of Katie Elder.

Three-year-old John Ethan Wayne visits his father on location during the filming of The Sons of Katie Elder.

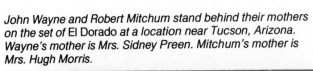

John Wayne and Robert Mitchum stand behind their mothers on the set of El Dorado *at a location near Tucson, Arizona. Wayne's mother is Mrs. Sidney Preen. Mitchum's mother is Mrs. Hugh Morris.*

Wayne and his son Patrick play chess between scenes of the 1965 film In Harm's Way.

Lucille Ball and John Wayne in a scene from The Lucy Show *which aired on CBS-TV in November, 1966.*

John Wayne shares a laugh with then-Congressman Gerald
Ford at the 16th annual National Football Foundation and
Hall of Fame Awards dinner in New York, December 4, 1973.
Wayne received the Foundation's Gold Medal award.

7
Without Reservations

Wayne was never a man to mince his words or mask his convictions. So when politics came upon the Hollywood scene, he waded into it straightforwardly, as he had gone into action against the bad guys on the screen. He never had any doubts about the rights and wrongs.

It all started in the late 1940s with the establishment of the Motion Picture Alliance for the Preservation of American Ideals, a group set up to defend the industry against communism.

Wayne became president of the Alliance in 1949 and served three terms during the contentious period of Senator Joseph McCarthy's Red-hunting days and the House Un-American Activities Committee's investigations into communist associations within the Hollywood set.

When actor Larry Parks admitted to once having been a Communist party member, reporters went to Wayne, as MPA president, for comment. Wayne allowed that it was too bad that Parks had been a Communist, but added it was courageous of him to admit it and he didn't believe a man who admits his mistakes should be made to pay again and again. He hoped Parks' confession wouldn't hurt his career.

His forgive-and-forget statement about Parks didn't go over too well with some other members of the Alliance, most notably its vice president, Hollywood gossip columnist Hedda Hopper.

At a mass meeting of the Alliance, she said Larry Parks certainly would not be forgiven, despite the statement of John Wayne.

"Well, you certainly gave it to me," Wayne said to Hedda with a grin after the meeting.

"Well, you certainly deserved it," Hedda replied.

Later, she told a friend, "Duke is a little dumb about these things."

Communists were indirectly involved in another Wayne incident, in 1959. It seemed that Wayne had gone into the shrimp-boat business in Panama, with Roberto Arias, son of a former Panamanian president. Wayne had put some half-million dollars into the venture.

Arias was later revealed to be the leader of a small band of rebels who tried an unsuccessful invasion coup, apparently copying Fidel Castro's guerrilla techniques. Some thought Wayne's money was used to support the revolutionary plot, but Wayne and Panamanian officials stressed the actor was in no way involved.

His Panamanian connections, which went back to his first marriage, got him into a little more hot water in 1978, when word got out that Wayne had sent a telegram to Panama's political boss, General Omar Torrijos, offering "best wishes for a good relationship between our countries." Wayne had had business and personal ties in Panama for forty years and he sent the message as a matter of "polite protocol," he said, not as an endorsement of the Panama Canal treaties.

96

Wayne takes time out from filming Universal's The War Wagon *in Durango, Mexico, to cast his absentee ballot for the gubernatorial California election. He supported Republican Ronald Reagan.*

His politically conservative fans apparently didn't take it that way, however, and let him know it.

"People started sending me letters that I'd fallen off my horse too many times," he said.

Despite his protestations about politics in general—he considered it a necessary evil—Wayne became a leading Hollywood voice of conservative Republicanism. He supported Arizona Senator Barry Goldwater and Presidents Eisenhower and Nixon.

In 1968 Wayne gave the opening speech at the Republican National Convention, a speech given largely to articulating his hopes and plans for his daughter.

He said he would want her "most of all to be grateful, as I am grateful, for every day of life I have spent in the United States of America."

In that year, too, there were rumors he would be George Wallace's vice-presidential running mate on the American Independent party ticket. Wayne denied it in unmistakable, if not unprintable, terms.

By 1972 he was already the elder statesman of the GOP box office parade and was asked to introduce a film on President Nixon at his renomination convention. Wayne was advised to introduce the film with the remark that Nixon is "a great president, and a good guy." But Wayne reversed the order of the phrases accidentally.

In the spring of 1972 Wayne returned to the USC campus, with Bob Hope, on the college lecture circuit. Wayne insisted on writing his own speech.

He pulled no punches, despite the "liberal" audience, and told the students of his displeasure with the radical fervor on the nation's campuses. He spoke about the university as a quiet place of learning, and he spoke about respect for the faculty and the institution.

"We are not going to let you destroy our schools," he told them.

At first there was some booing and heckling from the audience. But perhaps it was Wayne's honesty and straightforwardness that made a difference. As he spoke, they listened; he finished to a standing ovation.

He seemed to mute his political statements in later years, although he always had a few cracks to make about his critics in the "liberal" press.

About President Jimmy Carter, he would say only this, "I occasionally write him a critical note and occasionally he answers."

"I'm trying not to get involved," he would add. "I don't particularly care for politics—and not many politicians."

California's Republican Governor Ronald Reagan is flanked by Bob Hope, John Wayne, Dean Martin, and Frank Sinatra at a Los Angeles fund-raising rally during his reelection campaign in 1970.

John Wayne speaks after accepting his Gold Medal Award from the National Football Foundation and Hall of Fame in New York as Vice-president-designate Gerald Ford enjoys the occasion. Ford received the honor the year before in 1972.

Secretary of Transportation John A. Volpe adjusts the microphone as John Wayne makes a short speech to the Illinois caucus at the Republican National Convention in Miami Beach in August, 1972.

Wayne's brand of sincere (and, critics complained, unquestioning) patriotism led him into whole-hearted support of the war in Vietnam and he went there in 1966 for a three-week tour, during which he narrowly escaped injury from Viet Cong sniper fire. He came back determined—much as he'd been determined about *The Alamo*—to do a film about the war, "naturally from the hawk's point of view."

The idea of making a film about Vietnam in 1967 was about as unpopular as the war itself. Most studios shied away from the subject as box office poison. Indeed, *The Green Berets*—as he was to title it, based on the U.S. Special Forces—was first announced as a Universal production. Later, Wayne and his Batjac Productions moved the project to Warner Bros. "I guess those guys at Universal were scared of it," said Wayne.

Despite general corporate indifference, some army restrictions at the Fort Benning, Georgia, location, and the taunts of anti-Vietnam war protesters,

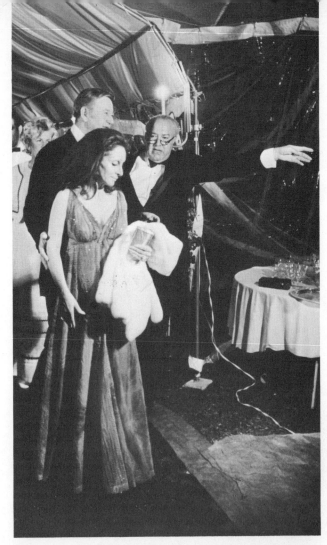

John and Pilar Wayne arrive at a dinner honoring former prisoners of war. A large tent was set up on the South Lawn of the White House for the May, 1973, affair.

John Wayne signs autographs during a trip to entertain U.S. troops in Vietnam in 1966. With him is Capt. Peter Dawkins, former Army football star and Rhodes Scholar.

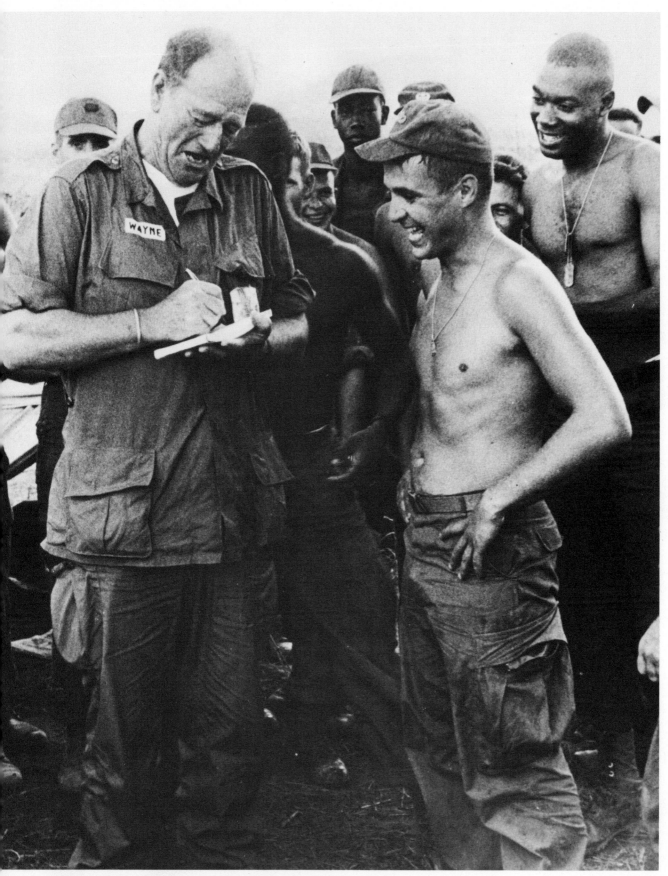

*Wearing combat fatigues, Wayne signs autographs while
visiting the 101st Airborne Division based at Dak To in South
Vietnam in 1966.*

Wayne covers a lot of distance by helicopter as he combines film business and visits with Vietnam casualties on Okinawa.

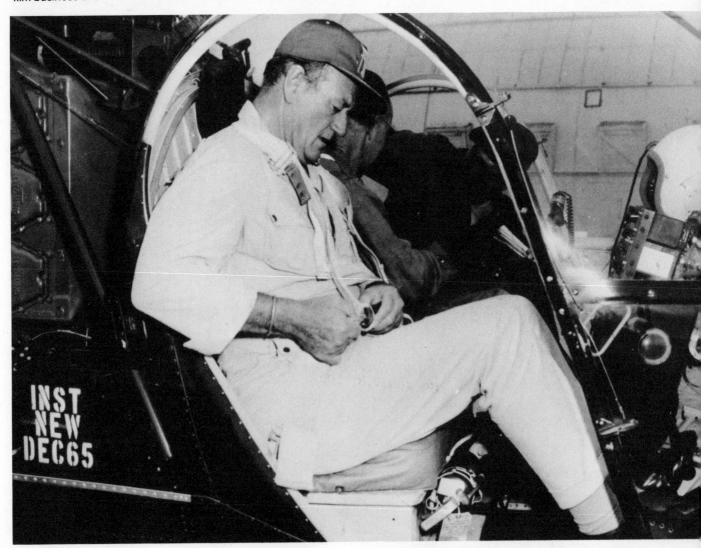

Wayne covers a lot of distance by helicopter as he combines film business and visits with Vietnam casualties on Okinawa.

INST
NEW
DEC65

the determined Wayne starred in and directed his film of the unpopular conflict.

His comments to the AP's Bob Thomas at the time revealed his feelings:

> What war hasn't been unpopular? Nobody's enjoying this war, but it happens to be damned necessary. If we hadn't gone into Vietnam, Indonesia wouldn't have been encouraged to beat the communists in their country. Thailand, which is the heart of the rice country in Southeast Asia, would have fallen to the communists.
>
> Ever since the revolution of 1917, the communists haven't compromised once in the family of nations. They're out to destroy us, and logic would tell us that this [the Vietnam War] is the right course.
>
> Besides, we gave our word. . . .
>
> For a number of years, we established a pretty good picture of America throughout the world with those pictures. But they don't seem to think of that nowadays.
>
> We received good treatment at Benning—within the letter of the law. We could use the army's equip-

> ment, if it wasn't tied up in training and could shoot in areas that weren't being used by troops. But the soldiers weren't available to us—unless they could get a two- or three-day pass. Then we paid them regular extra pay. . . .
>
> Seems to me that those who are against the war are an articulate minority who attract more attention than their numbers would warrant.
>
> Well, I suppose the so-called liberals will find some way to get at me. They did it with *The Alamo,* when they quoted me as saying anyone who didn't go to see the picture was unpatriotic. If they could get at me with *The Alamo,* they'll sure as hell find a way to do it with *Green Berets.*

Whether any conspiratorial "they" were involved or not, the picture was generally panned, both as film and as politics. But Wayne had made his statement, verbally and visually, and that was no less important to him than box office. He had spoken up, through his medium, in behalf of a patriotic cause as he saw it.

During his Okinawa tour Wayne looks over a map of the terrain in the Camp Hardy area with Col. Jonathan F. Ladd, left, commanding officer, U.S. Army 1st Special Forces Group. Lt. Col. Charles J. Hoyt, B Company commander, looks on.

He never wavered in that attitude, in his notion of loyalty to country, right or wrong, no matter what controversy his posititons brought. And there was praise as well as hostility. In 1971 the Freedom Foundation awarded Wayne its National Service Medal for his "consistent, unabashed loyalty to America and its ideals" and for his many visits to GIs in combat zones. Three years later he received the foundation's George Washington Award for his first record album, *America, Why I Love Her,* which later served as the basis for a Bicentennial book.

Neither his occasional political tribulations nor the pans of his Vietnam picture prevented Duke from bouncing back with renewed strength. Once again he showed, you might say, true grit.

Actor, director, and coproducer John Wayne calls out directions from a floodlight ladder while on location for The Green Berets *(Warner Bros. / Seven Arts, 1968).*

A touching scene with young Craig Jue from The Green Berets.

A group of Los Angeles Rams football players visit Duke on the set of The Green Berets. *(Left to right)* David Jones, Lamar Lundy, Roger Brown, and Merlin Olsen.

Wayne takes a look at the next shot on the Hollywood set of The Green Berets.

John Wayne with Kim Darby in *True Grit*.

8

Crowing Rooster

Marshal Reuben "Rooster" Cogburn. Fat. Old. A patch over one eye. Tough and gruff, drunken and endearing, cantankerous and courageous. It was John Wayne's best role of a lengthy career.

True Grit, with a screenplay by Marguerite Roberts from a best-selling book by Charles Portis, is a kind of frontier fable about a young girl (Kim Darby in the film) who seeks out a man with the guts to help her avenge her father's murder. It was directed by Henry Hathaway, who had worked with Wayne previously, first on *The Shepherd of the Hills* in 1941, then on *Legend of the Lost, North to Alaska, Circus World,* and *The Sons of Katie Elder.*

The elements melded together beautifully to create such memorable scenes as:

· A drunken Wayne, on the trail of the outlaw, falling off his horse and declaring that's where they'll camp for the night.

· The climactic shootout, with Wayne challenging the band of outlaws and getting in reply: "Bold talk from a one-eyed fat man!" Wayne puts action to his bold talk, warns the killer, "Fill your hand, you son of a bitch!" puts his horse's reins in his teeth, a rifle in one hand, a pistol in the other, and charges across the valley at them, bullets flying.

· Or the tender and prideful ending in which

Wayne rides off into the winter sunset, jumping a fence to prove that the "one-eyed fat man" still can do it.

One reviewer called the last scene "so fine it will probably become Wayne's cinematic epitaph." The critic, Vincent Canby of *The New York Times,* noted too: "It's the kind of performance that I found myself beginning to remember quite fondly, even before the movie was over."

Western film historian William K. Everson wrote:

Unexpectedly, Wayne, playing some scenes for pure comedy, does some of his best acting in any non-Ford Western. One scene in which he half-humorously, yet half-wistfully, describes his brief married life and the son who didn't like him, reveals a subtlety and an honest warmth in Wayne that has rarely been displayed before.

Wayne has said: "I guess that scene in *True Grit* is about the best I ever did."

Everson added:

With Gary Cooper gone, Wayne has not only become Hollywood's Western figurehead, but he is also still a box office giant. Obviously, he will go on making Westerns for as long as his expanding girth can stride a saddle. One can only hope that when he does decide to hang up his boots (if not his political guns), it will be with a vehicle as sympathetic and felicitous as *True Grit.*

A particularly fierce-looking closeup of Wayne in his Oscar-winning role as Sheriff Rooster Cogburn in True Grit *(Paramount, 1969).*

Wayne happily presents the Cecil B. DeMille Award to Joan Crawford at the Golden Globe Awards given by the Hollywood Foreign Press Association in California, February, 1970.

Wayne was nominated for a Best Actor Academy Award, along with some pretty impressive competitors: Dustin Hoffman, Peter O'Toole, Richard Burton, and Jon Voight.

He took a break from shooting *Rio Lobo,* with old director-friend Howard Hawks, to attend the Academy of Motion Picture Arts and Sciences award ceremony on April 7, 1970. It was an emotional moment when presenter Barbra Streisand opened the traditional envelope to announce:

"And for best performance by a male actor, the award goes to . . . John Wayne."

Duke Wayne, unabashedly wiping his moist eyes, accepted his first Oscar, after more than forty years in the business.

"I feel very grateful, very humble," he said, and, with the familiar grin, added:

"If I'd known what I know now, I'd have put a patch on my eye thirty-five years ago."

Although Duke Wayne had received many industry awards for his box office prowess, *True Grit* brought the first solid, official recognition of his talent as an actor. Acclaim gushed forth with a sudden surprising warmth, as if to make up for the long period of relative critical neglect.

Wrote movie critic Andrew Sarris after *True Grit*:

Wayne's performances for John Ford alone are worth all the Oscars passed out to the likes of George Arliss, Warner Baxter, Lionel Barrymore, Paul Lukas, Broderick Crawford, Jose Ferrer, Ernest Borgnine, Yul Brynner and David Niven.

Indeed, Wayne's performance in *The Searchers, Wings of Eagles,* and *The Man Who Shot Liberty Valance* are among the most full-bodied and large-souled creations of the cinema; and not too far behind are the characterizations in *She Wore a Yellow Ribbon, They Were Expendable, Fort Apache, Rio Grande, Three Godfathers, The Quiet Man, The Horse Soldiers, Donovan's Reef, Stagecoach* and *The Long Voyage Home.*

And that is only the Ford oeuvre.

Rio Bravo, El Dorado and *Red River* for Hawks are almost on the same level as the Ford and *Hatari* is not too far behind. Then there are the merely nice movies like *Reap the Wild Wind* (with Paulette Goddard), *The Spoilers* (with Marlene Dietrich), *The Lady Takes a Chance* (with Jean Arthur), *Tall in the Saddle* (with Ella Raines), *Wake of the Red Witch* (with Gail Russell), *The High and the Mighty.*

Finally, there are the leisurely Hathaway movies—*The Shepherd of the Hills, North to Alaska, The Sons of Katie Elder.*

No one has suggested that his acting range extends to Restoration fops and Elizabethan fools. But it would be a mistake to assume that all he can play or had played is the conventional Western gunfighter. . . . Wayne embodies the brutal, implacable order of the West, less with personal flair than with archetypical endurance. . . .

John Wayne and Anthony Quinn at the annual Hollywood Golden Globe awards dinner in Los Angeles, February, 1970.

Barbra Streisand congratulates Wayne as he accepts the Oscar for Best Actor for his role in True Grit.

Duke, with a firm grip on his Oscar, arrives with his wife, Pilar, at a party following the Academy Awards in April, 1970.

Ironically, Wayne has become a legend by not being legendary. He has dominated the screen even when he has not been written in as the dominant character.

One of those who knew how to get the best of Wayne's acting, Howard Hawks, was scarcely surprised. "John Wayne has just come to be recognized for the good actor that he is. I've always thought he was a good actor. I always thought he could do things that other people can't do," he said.

"If you try to make a Western with somebody besides Wayne, you're not in the sphere of violence and action that you are when you've got Wayne. I think that unless he is working with a damn good actor, he's going to blow them right off the screen.

"Not intentionally, just because he . . . he does it."

Wayne himself often discussed his craft and insisted he didn't "act," he "re-acted."

"I like basic-emotion stuff; nuance is out of my line. . . .You can't *be* natural; you have to *act* natural. And it's better to re-act than act."

At one time Wayne doubted he would ever win an

Oscar, partly because the roles he played did not generally call for the dramatic gamut that most often catches the Academy member vote. And he often expressed annoyance with those who belittled his acting ability.

Years ago he told AP columnist Hal Boyle:

"I wonder what they think acting is. I've been earning a living as an actor for more than twenty-five years. I don't go in for chi-chi or the dirty shirt school of acting. Perhaps nobody but another actor knows how difficult it is to play a straight character part."

His idea of acting, he said, was "merely to act by a code—the code of manhood. In any role, I try to act as any man or woman would think a real man ought to act in that situation. That's all. I merely try to act naturally, and without phoniness."

When Duke returned to Arizona, after the Academy Award ceremony, to complete *Rio Lobo,* he found an unusual and unusually heart-warming sight. Every member of the cast and crew, from director Howard Hawks to the fourth assistant prop man—even Wayne's horse—was wearing a patch over one eye.

John Wayne at the wheel of his boat in Mexico, February, 1969.

Wayne on location in Mexico in 1969.

Two-year-old Marisa Carmela enjoys a laugh with her father on the set of Hellfighters *in Hollywood, April, 1968.*

Eight-year-old John Ethan Wayne gets some tips on the acting profession from his father during filming of Rio Lobo *in Cuernavaca, Mexico.*

John Wayne, the father of seven and grandfather of nineteen, gets acquainted with two of the 1,040 Mexican orphans he adopted in Cuernavaca, Mexico, during the filming of Rio Lobo.

Wayne sings in a scene from his first television special filmed in Hollywood in 1970.

*Wayne trains the youngest hard-riding range hands in the
Old West in* The Cowboys *(Warner Bros., 1972).*

*Duke and one of his young sidekicks
in a scene from* The Cowboys.

John Wayne gets some tips from Dan Rowan (left) and Dick Martin (right) for "The Bunny Sketch," part of Rowan and Martin's Laugh-In television show, August, 1972.

Wayne stars as a freewheeling adventurer who agrees to help a young widow, played by Ann-Margret, in The Train Robbers (Warner Bros., 1973).

Wayne waves his hat to spectators as he rides in the lead car of the 1973 Rose Bowl Parade.

9
The Undefeated

"My public image has been quite heroic; I feel this like a country boy. I suppose that you tend to manage your life and your thinking in a manner that is expected. I would not want mine to be different.

"I try to live my life to the fullest without hurting anybody else. I try not to unintentionally hurt anybody's feelings. If I do hurt anybody's feelings, I had all the intentions of hurting them."

Thus, an answer to an interviewer's questions about John Wayne's philosophy on life, and, in a word, his description of it: "Exciting!"

"Since that cancer operation," he added, "it is awfully nice to wake up in the morning."

Questioned at that time about retiring, his reply was, "No desire at all. I really enjoy my work. You die if you retire, if not physically, mentally. A hard day's work still appeals to me."

An indeed it did, even after *True Grit.*

The Undefeated (Rock Hudson) and *Chisum; Rio Lobo; Big Jake* (with son John Ethan, then eight); *The Cowboys; The Train Robbers; Cahill, U.S. Marshal; McQ.*

In *McQ,* he was a detective, and a 1974 premiere of the movie provided another John Wayne anecdote—and insight. The *Harvard Lampoon,* a college humor magazine of national renown, noted Wayne's "unsurpassed greatness in the guts department" and dared him to premiere *McQ* in Harvard Square.

Wayne accepted, arriving in a tanklike personnel carrier that rumbled from the *Lampoon* offices to the theater. The proceedings were billed as an assault on the Eastern Liberal Establishment.

Wayne stood in the hatch, carrying an unloaded and inoperative gun, grinned, waved, handed out autographs and dodged snowballs tossed from Harvard dormitories. *Lampoon* staffers, dressed as cowboys and Keystone Kops, fired toy guns.

Then he did another detective story, *Brannigan,* and a reprise, *Rooster Cogburn,* with Katharine Hepburn, something of a combination *True Grit* with *African Queen.*

In 1976 he played an aging, cancer-ridden gunslinger who dies with his boots on in *The Shootist,* with Jimmy Stewart and Lauren Bacall. There were obvious questions about autobiographical parallels.

"Bull! It won't be my last film," Duke exclaimed on the Nevada location.

"Unless I stop breathing, or people stop going to see my films, I'll be making more of them."

It was during the filming of *The Shootist* that Wayne noticed his voice was getting hoarse.

"I couldn't figure out what was wrong," he said. "Neither could the doctors. I went to Frank Sinatra's

John Wayne rides to the opening of McQ atop an armored personnel carrier as Harvard students greet him along the route from the Harvard Lampoon office to Harvard Square.

John "Duke" Wayne meets Wayne Duke at a Rose Bowl luncheon in Pasadena, California, in 1972. Wayne was made grand marshal of the Tournament of Roses parade.

doctor. I went to the doctor of that other singer, the kid I used in *The Alamo*—what's his name? [Frankie Avalon.] They photographed my throat, but couldn't find anything."

He began feeling terribly weak and further tests disclosed a heart murmur. Surgery was indicated.

At age seventy, John Wayne underwent open-heart surgery at Massachusetts General Hospital in Boston.

"All of my children came back there to be with me, God bless them.

"The night before the surgery I asked if I could take them out to dinner. The doctors said I could. And could I have a drink? Yes, I could have one.

"So all of us went out to a restaurant that has been built inside the old city hall. They gave us a private dining room. When I walked in and saw the stained glass window and the table set for thirteen, I thought, 'It's the Last Supper!'

"If I can have only one drink, it's going to be the biggest damn drink you can pour!"

Wayne arrives at Heathrow Airport in London, January 17, 1974, to start filming McQ.

Director John Sturges watches as Wayne aims a new M10 9mm weapon on the set of McQ.

Duke towers over journalists and admirers at a press conference at London's Grosvenor House Hotel in 1974.

Wayne with his three-and-one-half-year-old grandson, Michael Ian Wayne, during a break in the shooting of Big Jake (National General, 1971).

(Left ro right) *Bob Hope, Frank Sinatra, Bing Crosby, and John Wayne prepare to tape a two-hour special,* Bob Hope's Quarter Century of Comedy, *at NBC in Los Angeles, California, October, 1975.*

The three-hour operation involved replacing a defective heart valve with a similar one from a pig. Wayne came through it in fine shape and with a bonus: His voice was back.

Wayne, who had separated from his third wife, Pilar, in 1973, went home to Newport Beach, beside Balboa Bay, to recuperate. He celebrated his seventy-first birthday, but it was not like the rip-roaring birthdays of the past.

"I keep thinking I'm well," he said on that May occasion just weeks after the operation, "but when I try too much I realize I'm not. When I do too much, I feel sore.

"You know, I still have only one lung; that's one thing you can't fix with pig valves."

Then he developed hepatitis. But, typically, it didn't stop him from keeping a work date, hosting a

Wayne as a tough-minded Chicago cop in the 1975 film Brannigan.

*John Wayne and Katharine Hepburn discuss a scene.from
Rooster Cogburn with director Stuart Millar. The movie is a
reprise of Wayne's Oscar-winning True Grit character.*

*Producer Hal B. Wallis discusses an upcoming action scene
with Duke on the Oregon location for Rooster Cogburn.*

General Electric one hundredth anniversary television special—and planning more films.

"I've got a big Western I'd like to do," he said. "They don't seem to be making Westerns now, but they'll come back."

Wayne turned to making other television specials for ABC and signed a $1.2 million three-year contract to do TV commercials for a California savings and loan company.

Then, on January 10, 1979, he entered UCLA Medical Center for a "routine" gallbladder operation. Two days later he had his stomach removed during a nine-and-one-half-hour operation when a cancerous tumor was discovered. Hospital representatives at first announced his prognosis was "excellent," but during the following week tissue tests revealed cancer in the gastric lymph nodes, "with the probability it will spread."

His oldest sons, Michael and Patrick, expressed confidence that their father would weather the latest ordeal, as he had before. "He's been down this road before and he's come back before," said Patrick. "Doctors had prepared us for this eventuality. It didn't come as a total shock."

Wayne's three sons—Michael, Patrick, and Ethan—and four daughters—Antonia, Melinda, Aissa, and Marisa—were at the medical center throughout the operation. Friends and a colorful assortment of fans kept a vigil at the hospital and prayed for "the Duke."

The hospital switchboard was deluged with inquiries from well-wishers, including calls from the personal secretary to Queen Elizabeth of Great Britain. President Carter, Queen Juliana of The Netherlands, Senator John Warner and his wife, actress Elizabeth Taylor, and Bob Hope were among those who sent get-well messages.

"They just want to say they're praying for the Duke and love him," a hospital representative said of the flood of telephone calls and bright bouquets of flowers that streamed in as well.

The outpouring of affection for one of Hollywood's enduring legends recalled the response to Wayne's heart surgery the year before, when he received more than 100,000 get-well messages.

Wayne said at the time: "There were 100,000 people asking the man upstairs to intercede for me. I can't tell you how much that meant to me."

Just days before he entered the hospital for what turned out to be cancer surgery, Duke was interviewed by Barbara Walters for an ABC television special. In the taped program he talked about life—and death—with characteristic courage and determination.

"My idea of a very good day," he said, "is getting up in the morning—and finding I'm still here."

John Wayne and Frank Sinatra at a reception prior to the television taping of An All-Star Tribute to John Wayne *in November, 1976, on ABC-TV.*

John Wayne and James Stewart at memorial services for Howard Hawks in Los Angeles, December, 1977.

Duke Wayne, Chuck Connors of The Rifleman, and Clayton Moore of The Lone Ranger, chat during rehearsal at ABC studios in Los Angeles for the network's Silver Anniversary aired February, 1978.

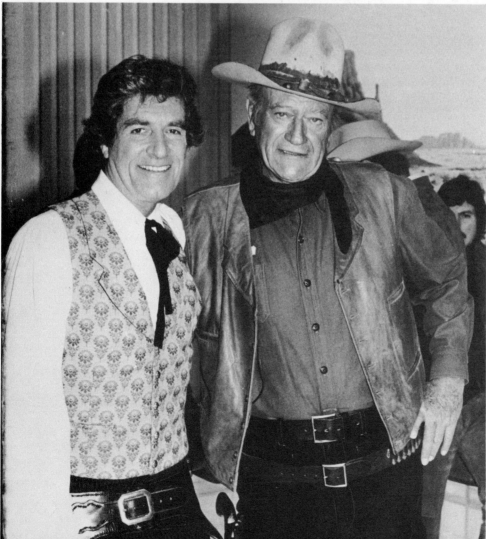

Hugh O'Brian and Wayne on the set of ABC's Silver Anniversary.

Asked how he felt about being called a "legend" in his own time, he grinned and replied: "They talk like you're part of the past. So I am. But I also want to be part of the future. . . .

"Listen, I spoke to the Man there on many occasions. I've always had deep faith that there is a Supreme Being. To me, that's just a normal thing, to have that kind of faith.

"The fact that He's let me stick around a little longer—or She let me stick around a little longer—certainly goes great with me. And I want to hang around as long as I'm healthy and not in anybody's way."

Exactly three months after his stomach cancer surgery, the indomitable Wayne walked on to center stage at the Los Angeles Music Center the night of April 10, 1979, to present the Best Picture Academy Award for *The Deer Hunter*.

When the lengthy and loving ovation subsided, Wayne commented, "That's just about the only medicine a fella'd ever really need. Believe me when I tell you I'm mighty pleased that I can amble down here tonight."

He looked gaunt—he had lost some forty pounds since the operation—but stood tall as he noted, "Oscar and I have something in common. Oscar first came to the Hollywood scene in 1928. So did I. We're both a little weather-beaten, but we're still here. And we plan to be around for a whole lot longer."

Illness finally vanquished John Wayne the man—but John Wayne the movie star lives on as a screen symbol of an American legend: the masculine, plain-talking man of action, quick with his hands or his gun, incorruptible, and always on the side of right.

Ten-year-old daughter Marisa gets a last-minute costume adjustment for her acting debut with her father in The Shootist.

John Wayne as an aging gunfighter in The Shootist. *(Paramount, 1976).*

An encouraging "Get Well Duke" sign appears on the baseball diamond across the street from Massachusetts General Hospital in Boston where Wayne was hospitalized for lung and heart problems.

Wayne talked openly about death over the years and, at such moments, liked to quote a Spanish proverb he thought wouldn't make a bad epitaph:

"*Feo, fuerte y formal.*"

"He was ugly, strong, and had dignity."

Something else comes to mind, from one of Wayne's better films, *She Wore a Yellow Ribbon*. Wayne played U.S. Cavalry Captain Nathan Brittles, about to retire after years of exceptional service.

Joanne Dru, who played the daughter of the commanding officer, watched the captain depart after his final mission. Her father told her gently that she shouldn't cry for him.

"I'm not crying," she replied

"I want to stand up and cheer."

Wayne waves to reporters at the Orange County Airport in Santa Ana, California, in April, 1978, on his return from Boston where he had undergone open-heart surgery three weeks earlier.

Duke is embraced by his daughters Melinda Munzo, left, and Aissa Wayne, right, as he leaves a private jet at Orange County Airport. Wayne, recovering from open-heart surgery, said, "I've got a close family, thank God."

Wayne's appearance at the Los Angeles Music Center on April 10, 1979, was one of the highlights of the Academy Awards festivities.

John Wayne, in familiar Western gear, discusses his Oscar for True Grit *and the contributions of other great Western stars in* Oscar's Best Actors *aired on ABC-TV in May, 1978.*

Wayne waves to fans as he enters the Beverly Hilton in
March, 1978, to attend award ceremonies for actor Henry
Fonda.

Filmography

MOTHER MACHREE. Fox 1928. Directed by John Ford. Cast: Belle Bennett, Neil Hamilton, Philippe De Lacy, Pat Somerset, Victor McLaglen. John Wayne is an unbilled extra in a story about an Irish mother in America and her son.

HANGMAN'S HOUSE. Fox 1928. Directed by John Ford. Cast: Victor McLaglen, Hobart Bosworth, June Collyer, Larry Kent, Earle Foxe, Eric Mayne, Joseph Burke, Belle Stoddard. John Wayne is an excited spectator at a horse race who smashes a picket fence in his enthusiasm.

SALUTE. Fox 1929. Directed by John Ford. Cast: George O'Brien, Helen Chandler, Stepin Fetchit, William Janney, Frank Albertson, Joyce Compton, Cliff Dempsey, Lumsden Hare, David Butler, Rex Bell, John Breeden, Ward Bond. John Wayne and Ward Bond are two of the football players in a story of Army-Navy rivalry. Wayne's first speaking role.

WORDS AND MUSIC. Fox 1929. Directed by James Tinling. Cast: Lois Moran, David Percy, Helen Twelvetrees, William Orlamond, Elizabeth Patterson, Frank Albertson, Tom Patricola, Bubbles Crowell, The Biltmore Quartet. Duke Morrison is the way John Wayne is billed in this musical of two college rivals competing for a campus coed.

MEN WITHOUT WOMEN. Fox 1930. Directed by John Ford. Cast: Kenneth MacKenna, Frank Albertson, Paul Page, Pat Somerset, Walter McGrail, Stuart Erwin, Warren Hymer, J. Farrell MacDonald, Roy Stewart, Warner Richmond, Harry Tenbrook, Ben Hendricks Jr., George LeGuere, Robert Parrish. John Wayne is one of fourteen men trapped in a submarine.

ROUGH ROMANCE. Fox 1930. Directed by A. F. Erickson. Cast: George O'Brien, Helen Chandler, Antonio Moreno, Noel Francis, Eddie Borden, Harry Cording, Roy Stewart, John Wayne. A Northwesterner.

CHEER UP AND SMILE. Fox 1930. Directed by Sidney Lanfield. Cast: Arthur Lake, Dixie Lee, Olga Baclanova, "Whispering" Jack Smith, Johnny Arthur, Charles Judels, John Darrow, Sumner Getchell, Franklin Pangborn, Buddy Messinger, John Wayne. A comedy-drama of youthful love affairs.

THE BIG TRAIL. Fox. 1930 Directed by Raoul Walsh. Cast: John Wayne, Marguerite Churchill, El Brendel, Tully Marshall, Tyrone Power Sr., David Rollins, Frederick Burton, Russ Powell, Ward Bond, Marcia Harris, Andy Shufford, Helen Parrish. Wayne, in his first featured role, is a frontier scout in a story of the old Oregon Trail.

GIRLS DEMAND EXCITEMENT. Fox 1931. Directed by Seymour Felix. Cast: Virginia Cherrill, John Wayne, Marguerite Churchill, Helen Jerome Eddy, William Janney, Eddie Nugent, Terrance Ray, Marion Byron, Martha Sleeper, Addie McPhail, Ray Cooke. Wayne is leader of the boys at a coed university; he captains the basketball team in a rivalry with the girls' team.

THREE GIRLS LOST. Fox 1931. Directed by Sidney Lanfield. Cast: Loretta Young, John Wayne, Lew Cody, Joyce Compton, Joan Marsh, Katherine Clare Ward, Paul Fix, Bert Roach. Wayne is a struggling young architect in love with Joan Marsh in a story of three girls who come to the city seeking fame and fortune.

MEN ARE LIKE THAT. Columbia 1931. Directed by George B. Seitz. Cast: John Wayne, Laura LaPlante, June Clyde, Forrest Stanley, Nena Quartaro, Susan Fleming, Loretta Sayers, Hugh Cummings. A romance, with Wayne in army uniform as a West Point graduate assigned to a post in Arizona.

RANGE FEUD. Columbia 1931. Directed by D. Ross Lederman. Cast: Buck Jones, John Wayne, Susan Fleming, Ed LeSaint, William Walling, Wallace MacDonald, Harry Woods. A Western in which Wayne is a rancher's son falsely accused of killing a rival rancher.

MAKER OF MEN. Columbia 1931. Directed by Edward Sedgwick. Cast: Jack Holt, Richard Cromwell, Joan Marsh, Robert Alden, John Wayne, Walter Catlett, Natalie Moorehead, Ethel Wales, Richard Tucker, Mike McKay. Wayne is a college football player.

SHADOW OF THE EAGLE. Mascot 1932. Directed by Ford Beebe. Cast: John Wayne, Dorothy Gulliver, Edward Hearn, Richard Tucker, Lloyd Whitlock, Walter Miller, Edmund Burns, Pat O'Malley, Little Billy, Ivan Linow, James Bradbury Jr., Ernie S. Adams, Roy D'Arcy, Bud Osborne, Yakima Canutt. A twelve-chapter serial in which Wayne plays an airplane pilot.

THE HURRICANE EXPRESS. Mascot 1932. Directed by Armand Schaefer and J. P. McGowan. Cast: John Wayne, Shirley Grey, Tully Marshall, Conway Tearle, J. Farrell MacDonald, Matthew Betz, James Burtis, Lloyd Whitlock, Edmund Breese, Al Bridge, Ernie S. Adams, Charles King, Glenn Strange. A twelve-chapter serial in which Wayne plays an air transport pilot who tracks down the cause of a series of mysterious train wrecks, one of which killed his father.

HAUNTED GOLD. Warner Bros. 1932. Directed by Mack V. Wright. Cast: John Wayne, Sheila Terry, Erville Alderson, Harry Woods, Otto Hoffman, Martha Mattox, Blue Washington. Wayne fights an outlaw gang for an abandoned, and haunted, gold mine.

TEXAS CYCLONE. Columbia 1932. Directed by D. Ross Lederman. Cast: Tim McCoy, Shirley Grey, John Wayne, Wheeler Oakman, Wallace MacDonald, Harry Cording, Vernon Dent, Walter Brennan, Mary Gordon. A Western.

LADY AND GENT. Paramount 1932. Directed by Stephen Roberts. Cast: George Bancroft, Wynne Gibson, Charles Starrett, James Gleason, John Wayne, Joyce Compton, Charles Grapewin, Frank McGlynn Sr. Wayne is a young prizefighter.

Stagecoach: *Claire Trevor, John Wayne.*

Pittsburgh: *Marlene Dietrich, John Wayne.*

Without Reservations: *John Wayne, Claudette Colbert.*

TWO FISTED LAW. Columbia 1932. Directed by D. Ross Lederman. Cast: Tim McCoy, Alice Day, Wheeler Oakman, Tully Marshall, Wallace MacDonald, John Wayne, Walter Brennan, Richard Alexander. A Western about a crooked cattleman.

RIDE HIM COWBOY. Warner Bros. 1932. Directed by Fred Allen. Cast: John Wayne, Ruth Hall, Henry B. Walthall, Harry Gribbon, Otis Harlan, Charles Sellon, Frank Hagney. Wayne saves "Duke"—a horse—from false charges of killing a rancher, and finds the real killer.

THE BIG STAMPEDE. Warner Bros. 1932. Directed by Tenny Wright. Cast: John Wayne, Noah Beery, Mae Madison, Luis Alberni, Berton Churchill, Paul Hurst. Wayne is a deputy sheriff after a cattle rustler.

THE TELEGRAPH TRAIL. Warner Bros. 1933. Directed by Tenny Wright. Cast: John Wayne, Marceline Day, Frank McHugh, Otis Harlan, Yakima Canutt, Albert J. Smith, Clarence

Geldert. Wayne is a government scout who leads the supply train through to the telegraph line workers.

HIS PRIVATE SECRETARY. Showmen's Pictures 1933. Directed by Philip H. Whitman. Cast: John Wayne, Evalyn Knapp, Alec B. Francis, Natalie Kingston, Arthur Hoyt, Al "Fuzzy" St. John, Mickey Rentschler. Wayne is a rich man's son with his mind on women.

CENTRAL AIRPORT. Warner Bros. 1933. Directed by William A. Wellman. Cast: Richard Barthelmess, Sally Eilers, Tom Brown, Glenda Farrell, Harold Huber, Grant Mitchell, James Murray, Claire McDowell, Willard Robertson, John Wayne. Wayne has a small part in an aviator romance.

SOMEWHERE IN SONORA. Warner Bros. 1933. Directed by Mack V. Wright. Cast: John Wayne, Shirley Palmer, Henry B. Walthall, Paul Fix, Ann Faye, Billy Franey, Ralph Lewis, Frank Rice, J. P. McGowan. A Western involving a lost son taken into an outlaw gang.

THE LIFE OF JIMMY DOLAN. Warner Bros. 1933. Directed by Archie Mayo. Cast: Douglas Fairbanks Jr., Loretta Young, Aline MacMahon, Guy Kibbee, Fifi D'Orsay, Shirley Grey, Lyle Talbot, Harold Huber, George Meeker, Mickey Rooney, John Wayne. Wayne has a bit part as a prizefighter.

BABY FACE. Warner Bros. 1933. Directed by Alfred E. Green. Cast: Barbara Stanwyck, George Brent, Donald Cook, Margaret Lindsay, Henry Kolker, John Wayne, Douglas Dumbrille, Arthur Hohl, Theresa Harris. Wayne has a bit part as a department store floorwalker.

THE MAN FROM MONTEREY. Warner Bros. 1933. Directed by Mack V. Wright. Cast: John Wayne, Ruth Hall, Nena Quartaro, Luis Alberni, Francis Ford, Donald Reed. Wayne is a U. S. captain who defeats swindlers in Monterey.

RIDERS OF DESTINY. Monogram 1933. Directed by Robert N. Bradbury. Cast: John Wayne, Cecilia Parker, George "Gabby" Hayes, Forrest Taylor, Al "Fuzzy" St. John. Wayne is an undercover agent who helps ranchers get their water rights.

SAGEBRUSH TRAIL. Monogram 1933. Directed by Armand Schaefer. Cast: John Wayne, Nancy Shubert, Lane Chandler, Yakima Canutt, Wally Wales, Art Mix. Wayne escapes from prison to find the real killer.

THE THREE MUSKETEERS. Mascot 1933. Directed by Armand Schaefer and Colbert Clark. Cast: John Wayne, Ruth Hall, Jack Mulhall, Raymond Hatton, Francis X. Bushman Jr., Noah Beery Jr., Creighton Chaney, Al Ferguson. In this twelve-chapter serial, Wayne is a latter-day Musketeer, an American Legionnaire in the Arab desert.

WEST OF THE DIVIDE. Monogram 1934. Directed by Robert N. Bradbury. Cast: John Wayne, Virginia Brown Faire, Lloyd Whitlock, George "Gabby" Hayes, Yakima Canutt. Wayne returns to his family ranch to find his father's killer and locate his missing brother.

THE LUCKY TEXAN. Monogram 1934. Directed by Robert N. Bradbury. Cast: John Wayne, Barbara Sheldon, George "Gabby" Hayes, Lloyd Whitlock, Yakima Canutt. Wayne and Gabby Hayes find gold.

BLUE STEEL. Monogram 1934. Directed by Robert N. Bradbury. Cast: John Wayne, Eleanor Hunt, George "Gabby" Hayes, Ed Peil, Yakima Canutt. Wayne is an undercover U. S. marshal who saves the town from an outlaw plot.

THE MAN FROM UTAH. Monogram 1934. Directed by Robert N. Bradbury. Cast: John Wayne, Polly Ann Young, George "Gabby" Hayes, Yakima Canutt, Ed Peil, Lafe McKee. Wayne is a deputy sheriff who uncovers a rodeo gang.

RANDY RIDES ALONE. Monogram 1934. Directed by Harry Fraser. Cast: John Wayne, Albert Vaughn, George "Gabby"

Hayes, Earl Dwire, Yakima Canutt. Wayne captures the gang which had been robbing the local express company.

THE STAR PACKER. Monogram 1934. Directed by Robert N. Bradbury. Cast: John Wayne, Verna Hillie, George "Gabby" Hayes, Yakima Canutt, Earl Dwire, Arthur Ortega. Wayne organizes the ranchers and defeats the gang.

THE TRAIL BEYOND. Monogram 1934. Directed by Robert N. Bradbury. Cast: John Wayne, Verna Hillie, Noah Beery, Iris Lancaster, Noah Beery Jr., Robert Frazer, Earl Dwire, Edward Parker. Wayne saves the girl and the gold mine from a gang.

'NEATH ARIZONA SKIES. Monogram 1934. Directed by Harry Fraser. Cast: John Wayne, Sheila Terry, Jay Wilsey, Yakima Canutt, Jack Rockwell, Shirley Ricketts, George "Gabby" Hayes. Wayne rescues an Indian girl from a gang of kidnappers and saves her father.

THE LAWLESS FRONTIER. Monogram 1934. Directed by Robert N. Bradbury. Cast: John Wayne, Sheila Terry, George "Gabby" Hayes, Earl Dwire, Yakima Canutt, Jack Rockwell. Wayne rounds up the outlaw gang to clear his name.

TEXAS TERROR. Monogram 1935. Directed by Robert N. Bradbury. Cast: John Wayne, Lucille Browne, LeRoy Mason, George "Gabby" Hayes, "Buffalo Bill" Cody Jr. Wayne finds the killer of his best friend.

RAINBOW VALLEY. Monogram 1935. Directed by Robert N. Bradbury. Cast: John Wayne, Lucille Brown, LeRoy Mason, George "Gabby" Hayes, "Buffalo Bill" Cody Jr., Bert Dillard, Lloyd Ingraham. Wayne goes to prison as an undercover agent.

PARADISE CANYON. Monogram 1935. Directed by Carl Pierson. Cast: John Wayne, Marion Burns, Yakima Canutt, Reed Howes, Perry Murdock, Gino Corrado, Gordon Clifford, Earl Hodgins. Wayne is an undercover agent who captures counterfeiters operating near the Mexican border.

THE DAWN RIDER. Republic 1935. Directed by Robert N. Bradbury. Cast: John Wayne, Marion Burns, Yakima Canutt, Reed Howes, Denny Meadows, Bert Dillard, Jack Jones. Wayne captures the killers of his father.

THE DESERT TRAIL. Republic 1935. Directed by Cullen Lewis. Cast: John Wayne, Mary Kornman, Paul Fix, Edward Chandler, Lafe McKee, Henry Hall. Wayne is a rodeo performer who captures holdup bandits.

WESTWARD HO. Republic 1935. Directed by Robert N. Bradbury. Cast: John Wayne, Sheila Manners, Frank McGlynn Jr., Jack Curtis, Yakima Canutt, Mary McLaren, Dickie Jones, Hank Bell. Wayne fights a gang that killed his parents, only to find his brother is involved.

THE NEW FRONTIER. Republic 1935. Directed by Carl Pierson. Cast: John Wayne, Muriel Evans, Mary McLaren,

The Fighting Kentuckian: *Vera Ralston, John Wayne.*

Murdock MacQuarrie, Warner Richmond, Sam Flint, Earl Dwire, Alfred Bridge. Wayne, as one of the Three Mesquiteers, helps ranchers fight for their land.

THE LAWLESS RANGE. Republic 1935. Directed by Robert N. Bradbury. Cast: John Wayne, Sheila Manners, Earl Dwire, Frank McGlynn Jr., Jack Curtis, Yakima Canutt. Wayne is an undercover agent involved with hidden gold mines.

THE LAWLESS NINETIES. Republic 1936. Directed by Joseph Kane. Cast: John Wayne, Ann Rutherford, Lane Chandler, Harry Woods, George "Gabby" Hayes, Etta McDaniel. Wayne is an undercover government agent who breaks up a terrorizing gang.

KING OF THE PECOS. Republic 1936. Directed by Joseph Kane. Cast: John Wayne, Muriel Evans, Cy Kendall, Jack Clifford, Frank Glendon, Herbert Heywood, Mary McLaren, Yakima Canutt. Wayne is a young lawyer who returns to his family's Texas land in the 1870s to reclaim it from a murdering cattle baron.

THE OREGON TRAIL. Republic 1936. Directed by Scott Pembroke. Cast: John Wayne, Ann Rutherford, Yakima Canutt, E. H. Calvert, Fern Emmett, Gino Corrado. Wayne and Spanish soldiers capture renegade frontiersmen.

WINDS OF THE WASTELAND. Republic 1936. Directed by Mack V. Wright. Cast: John Wayne, Phyllis Fraser, Yakima Canutt, Lane Chandler, Sam Flint, Lew Kelly, Bob Kortman, Douglas Cosgrove. Wayne buys a stagecoach and beats a rival in a race for a government mail contract.

THE SEA SPOILERS. Universal 1936. Directed by Frank Strayer. Cast: John Wayne, Nan Grey, Fuzzy Knight, William Bakewell, Russell Hicks, George Irving. Wayne commands a U. S. Coast Guard cutter and defeats a band of poachers and smugglers.

THE LONELY TRAIL. Republic 1936. Directed by Joseph Kane. Cast: John Wayne, Ann Rutherford, Cy Kendall, Snowflake, Etta McDaniel, Bob Kortman, Sam Flint, Yakima Canutt, Bob Burns. Wayne helps the governor get rid of carpetbaggers in post-Civil War Texas.

CONFLICT. Universal 1936. Directed by David Howard. Cast: John Wayne, Jean Rogers, Tommy Bupp, Eddie Borden, Ward Bond, Harry Woods. Wayne is a lumberjack-prizefighter.

CALIFORNIA STRAIGHT AHEAD. Universal 1937. Directed by Arthur Lubin. Cast: John Wayne, Louise Latimer, Robert McWade, Tully Marshall, Theodore von Eltz, LeRoy Mason, Grace Goodall. Wayne is a truck driver in a contest for delivery of aviation parts to an ocean liner.

I COVER THE WAR. Universal 1937. Directed by Arthur Lubin. Cast: John Wayne, Gwen Gaze, Don Barclay, James Bush, Pat Somerset, Charles Brokaw. Wayne is a newsreel cameraman in a desert hotbed of tribal unrest.

IDOL OF THE CROWDS. Universal 1937. Directed by Arthur Lubin. Cast: John Wayne, Sheila Bromley, Billy Burrud, Russell Hopton, Huntley Gordon, Charles Brokaw. Wayne is a professional hockey player.

ADVENTURE'S END. Universal 1937. Directed by Arthur Lubin. Cast: John Wayne, Diana Gibson, Moroni Olsen, Montague Love, Ben Carter, Maurice Black, George Cleveland, Glenn Strange, Britt Wood. Wayne survives a mutiny aboard a whaler.

BORN TO THE WEST. Paramount 1937. Directed by Charles Barton. Cast: John Wayne, Marsha Hunt, Johnny Mack Brown, John Patterson, Monte Blue, Lucien Littlefield, Alan Ladd, James Craig, Nick Lukats. Wayne leads a cattle drive and fights the rustlers.

PALS OF THE SADDLE. Republic 1938. Directed by George Sherman. Cast: John Wayne, Ray "Crash" Corrigan, Max Terhune, Doreen McKay, Frank Milan, Jack Kirk, Ted Adams, Harry Depp. Wayne, as one of the Three Mesquiteers, helps the government against a munitions ring.

OVERLAND STAGE RAIDERS. Republic 1938. Directed by George Sherman. Cast: John Wayne, Ray "Crash" Corrigan, Max Terhune, Louise Brooks, Fern Emmett, Frank LaRue, Anthony Marsh, Gordon Hart. Wayne and the other Mesquiteers ship gold by plane, foiling hijackers.

SANTA FE STAMPEDE. Republic 1938. Directed by George Sherman. Cast: John Wayne, Ray "Crash" Corrigan, Max Terhune, June Martel, William Farnum, LeRoy Mason, Martin Spellman, Tom London. The Three Mesquiteers help a gold miner.

RED RIVER RANGE. Republic 1938. Directed by George Sherman. Cast: John Wayne, Ray "Crash" Corrigan, Max Terhune, Polly Moran, Kirby Grant, William Royale, Perry Ivins, Stanley Blystone, Lenore Bushman. The Three Mesquiteers fight rustlers.

STAGECOACH. United Artists 1939. Directed by John Ford. Produced by Walter Wanger. Screenplay by Dudley Nichols, from "Stage to Lordsburg," by Ernest Haycox. Cast: John Wayne, Claire Trevor, John Carradine, Thomas Mitchell, Andy Devine, Donald Meek, Louise Platt, Tim Holt, George Bancroft, Berton Churchill, Tom Tyler, Chris Pin Martin, Elvira Rios, Francis Ford, Marga Ann Daighton, Kent Odell, Yakima Canutt, Chief Big Tree, Harry Tenbrook, Jack Pennick, Paul McVey, Cornelius Keefe, Florence Lake, Louis Mason, Brenda Fowler. Wayne is the Ringo Kid, one of a group of misfits and outcasts on the stage from Tonto to Lordsburg. He falls in love with Dallas (Claire Trevor), a café dancer who has been run out of town, helps fight off an Indian attack, and shoots it out with a gang of desperadoes in town. Ford's first Western to be shot in Monument Valley, as well as other locations in Arizona, Utah, and California. Academy Awards went to the composers and to Thomas Mitchell for Supporting Actor (as Dr. Josiah Boone).

The Sands of Iwo Jima: *Capt. H. G. Schrier, John Wayne, Jim Brown, Forrest Tucker.*

THE NIGHT RIDERS. Republic 1939. Directed by George Sherman. Cast: John Wayne, Ray "Crash" Corrigan, Max Terhune, Doreen McKay, Ruth Rogers, Tom Tyler, Kermit Maynard, George Douglas. The Three Mesquiteers defeat a powerful cardsharp cheat in the Southwest.

THREE TEXAS STEERS. Republic 1939. Directed by George Sherman. Cast: John Wayne, Ray "Crash" Corrigan, Max Terhune, Carole Landis, Ralph Graves, Collette Lyons, Roscoe Ates, Lew Kelly, David Sharpe. The Three Mesquiteers save a circus and a ranch for Carole Landis.

WYOMING OUTLAW. Republic 1939. Directed by George Sherman. Cast: John Wayne, Adele Pearce, Ray "Crash" Corrigan, Donald Barry, Raymond Hatton, LeRoy Mason, Yakima Canutt, Elmo Lincoln. The Three Mesquiteers uncover a crooked local politician.

NEW FRONTIER. Republic 1939. Directed by George Sherman. Cast: John Wayne, Ray "Crash" Corrigan, Raymond Hatton, Phyllis Isley (Jennifer Jones), Eddy Waller. The Three Mesquiteers save the settlers from land grabbers.

ALLEGHENY UPRISING. RKO Radio 1939. Directed by William A. Seiter. Cast: Claire Trevor, John Wayne, George Sanders, Brian Donlevy, Wilfrid Lawson, Robert Barrat, John F. Hamilton, Moroni Olsen, Eddie Quillan, Chill Wills. Wayne is a frontiersman battling Pennsylvania Indians and traders supplying them with firearms and liquor.

THE DARK COMMAND. Republic 1940. Directed by Raoul Walsh. Cast: John Wayne, Claire Trevor, Walter Pidgeon, Roy Rogers, George "Gabby" Hayes, Marjorie Main. Cowboy Wayne becomes federal marshal in Kansas before the Civil War.

THREE FACES WEST. Republic 1940. Directed by Bernard Vorhaus. Cast: John Wayne, Sigrid Gurie, Charles Coburn, Spencer Charters, Helen MacKellar, Roland Varno. Dust Bowl farmer Wayne leads a migration to Oregon and finds love.

THE LONG VOYAGE HOME. United Artists 1940. Directed by John Ford. Produced by Walter Wanger. Screenplay by Dudley Nichols from one-act plays by Eugene O'Neill. Cast: John Wayne, Thomas Mitchell, Ian Hunter, Barry Fitzgerald, Wilfrid

Rio Grande: *John Wayne and his son, twelve-year-old Pat Wayne.*

Lawson, Mildred Natwick, John Qualen, Ward Bond, Joe Sawyer, Arthur Shields, J. M. Kerrigan, David Hughes, Billy Bevan, Cyril McLaglen, Robert E. Perry, Jack Pennick. Wayne plays Ole Olson, sailor on the *Glencairn*.

SEVEN SINNERS. Universal 1940. Directed by Tay Garnett. Cast: John Wayne, Marlene Dietrich, Broderick Crawford, Mischa Auer, Albert Dekker, Billy Gilbert, Anna Lee, Oscar Homolka, Samuel S. Hinds, Reginald Denny. Wayne is a navy lieutenant on a South Sea island where Marlene Dietrich (Bijou) is a café singer.

A MAN BETRAYED. Republic 1941. Directed by John H. Auer. Cast: John Wayne, Frances Dee, Edward Ellis, Wallace Ford, Ward Bond, Harold Huber, Alexander Granach, Barnett Parker. Wayne is a small-town lawyer investigating the mysterious death of his close friend.

LADY FROM LOUISIANA. Republic 1941. Directed by Bernard Vorhaus. Cast: John Wayne, Ona Munson, Ray Middleton, Henry Stephenson, Helen Westley, Jack Pennick, Dorothy Dandridge. Wayne is a young lawyer fighting a crooked lottery in New Orleans.

THE SHEPHERD OF THE HILLS. Paramount 1941. Directed by Henry Hathaway. Cast: John Wayne, Betty Field, Harry Carey, Beulah Bondi, James Barton, Samuel S. Hinds, Marjorie Main, Ward Bond, Marc Lawrence, John Qualen, Fuzzy Knight, Tom Fadden. Wayne is an Ozark mountaineer who hates his father, but they wind up reconciled.

LADY FOR A NIGHT. Republic 1942. Directed by Leigh Jason. Cast: John Wayne, Joan Blondell, Ray Middleton, Philip Merivale, Blanche Yurka, Edith Barrett, Leonid Kinskey. Wayne is a Mississippi gambler.

REAP THE WILD WIND. Paramount 1942. Produced and directed by Cecil B. DeMille. Cast: Ray Milland, John Wayne, Paulette Goddard, Raymond Massey, Robert Preston, Lynne Overman, Susan Hayward, Charles Bickford, Walter Hampden, Louis Beavers, Martha O'Driscoll, Elizabeth Risdon, Hedda Hopper, Victor Kilian, Oscar Polk, Janet Beecher, Ben Carter. Wayne is a ship captain involved with pirates, undersea monsters, and Paulette Goddard.

THE SPOILERS. Universal 1942. Directed by Ray Enright. Cast: John Wayne, Marlene Dietrich, Randolph Scott, Margaret Lindsay, Harry Carey, Richard Barthelmess, William Farnum, George Cleveland, Samuel S. Hinds, Jack Norton. Wayne is part owner of an Alaskan gold mine, falsely accused of murder.

IN OLD CALIFORNIA. Republic 1942. Directed by William McGann. Cast: John Wayne, Binnie Barnes, Albert Dekker, Helen Parrish, Patsy Kelly, Edgar Kennedy, Dick Purcell, Harry Shannon. Wayne is a Boston pharmacist who journeys out West in frontier days to open a drugstore in Sacramento.

FLYING TIGERS. Republic 1942. Directed by David Miller. Cast: John Wayne, John Carroll, Anna Lee, Paul Kelly, Gordon Jones, Mae Clarke, Addison Richards, Tom Neal. Wayne is squadron leader Jim Gordon of the World War II Flying Tigers, fighting for China against the Japanese.

REUNION IN FRANCE. Metro-Goldwyn-Mayer 1942. Directed by Jules Dassin. Cast: John Wayne, Joan Crawford, Philip Dorn, Reginald Owen, Albert Basserman, John Carradine, Ann Ayars, Moroni Olsen, J. Edward Bromberg, Henry Daniell, Howard Da Silva, Ava Gardner. Wayne is an American flier shot down in Nazi-occupied France.

PITTSBURGH. Universal 1942. Directed by Lewis Seiler. Cast: John Wayne, Marlene Dietrich, Randolph Scott, Frank Craven, Louise Allbritton, Thomas Gomez, Paul Fix. Wayne plays a profiteering coal mine operator changed by the war.

A LADY TAKES A CHANCE. RKO Radio 1943. Directed by William A. Seiter. Cast: John Wayne, Jean Arthur, Charles Winninger, Phil Silvers, Mary Field, Don Costello, Grady Sutton, Grant Withers, Hans Conreid. Wayne is a rodeo rider in a high comedy-romance with Jean Arthur.

WAR OF THE WILDCATS. Republic 1943. Directed by Albert S. Rogell. Cast: John Wayne, Martha Scott, Albert Dekker, George "Gabby" Hayes, Marjorie Rambeau, Dale Evans, Grant Withers, Sidney Blackmer, Paul Fix. Cowboy Wayne and oil operator Dekker fight over Martha Scott.

Trouble Along the Way: *John Wayne.*

Legend of the Lost: *Sophia Loren, John Wayne.*

THE FIGHTING SEABEES. Republic 1944. Directed by Edward Ludwig and Howard Lydecker. Cast: John Wayne, Susan Hayward, Dennis O'Keefe, William Frawley, Addison Richards, Leonid Kinskey, Paul Fix, Grant Withers, Duncan Renaldo. Wayne is chief of the construction engineers in the Pacific during the war, sacrificing his life to save other Americans and an oil depot.

TALL IN THE SADDLE. RKO Radio 1944. Directed by Edwin L. Marin. Cast: John Wayne, Ella Raines, Ward Bond, George "Gabby" Hayes, Audrey Long, Elizabeth Risdon, Paul Fix, Raymond Hatton. A frontier Western written by Wayne's old friend Paul Fix, with Michael Hogan.

FLAME OF THE BARBARY COAST. Republic 1945. Directed by associate producer Joseph Kane. Cast: John Wayne, Ann Dvorak, Joseph Schildkraut, William Frawley, Virginia Grey, Russell Hicks, Jack Norton, Paul Fix, Manart Kippen, Eve Lynne, Marc Lawrence, Butterfly McQueen. Wayne plays Montana cattleman Duke Fergus, involved with San Francisco gamblers, an earthquake, and the Flame of the Barbary Coast, Ann Dvorak.

BACK TO BATAAN. RKO Radio 1945. Directed by Edward Dmytryk. Cast: John Wayne, Anthony Quinn, Beulah Bondi, Fely Franquelli, Leonard Strong, Richard Loo, Philip Ahn, Lawrence Tierney, Paul Fix, Abner Biberman, Vladimir Sokoloff. Wayne is Colonel Joseph Madden, fighting with the Filipino underground.

DAKOTA. Republic 1945. Directed by associate producer Joseph Kane. Cast: John Wayne, Vera Hruba Ralston, Walter Brennan, Ward Bond, Ona Munson, Hugo Haas, Mike Mazurki, Olive Blakeney, Paul Fix, Grant Withers, Jack LaRue. Land war in North Dakota.

THEY WERE EXPENDABLE. Metro-Goldwyn-Mayer 1945. Produced and directed by John Ford. Cast: Robert Montgomery, John Wayne, Donna Reed, Jack Holt, Ward Bond, Louis Jean Heydt, Marshall Thompson, Russell Simpson, Leon Ames, Paul Langton, Arthur Walsh, Donald Curtis, Cameron Mitchell. Wayne is Lieutenant Rusty Ryan in the story of the men who pioneered the use of the PT boat in combat, told against the backdrop of American defeats in the Philippines.

WITHOUT RESERVATIONS. RKO Radio 1946. Directed by Mervyn LeRoy. Cast: John Wayne, Claudette Colbert, Don DeFore, Anne Triola, Phil Brown, Frank Puglia, Dona Drake. High comedy aboard a train.

The Alamo: *Richard Widmark, Laurence Harvey, John Wayne.*

The Longest Day: *John Wayne*

ANGEL AND THE BADMAN. Republic 1947. Directed and written by James Edward Grant. Cast: John Wayne, Gail Russell, Harry Carey, Bruce Cabot, Irene Rich, Lee Dixon, Tom Powers, John Halloran, Stephen Grant. Wayne's first production. Gunfighter Wayne is converted by Quaker Gail Russell.

TYCOON. RKO Radio 1947. Directed by Richard Wallace. Cast: John Wayne, Laraine Day, Sir Cedric Hardwicke, Judith Anderson, James Gleason, Anthony Quinn, Grant Withers, Paul Fix. Wayne is an engineer building a railroad in the Andes.

FORT APACHE. RKO Radio 1948. Directed by John Ford. (Coproduced by Ford and Merian C. Cooper.) Cast: John Wayne, Henry Fonda, Shirley Temple, John Agar, Ward Bond, George O'Brien, Victor McLaglen, Pedro Armendariz, Anna Lee, Irene Rich, Guy Kibbee, Grant Withers, Miguel Inclan, Jack Pennick, Mae Marsh, Dick Foran, Frank Ferguson, Francis Ford. An arrogant and bitter lieutenant colonel (Henry Fonda) leads his men into an Apache massacre, but Captain Kirby York (Wayne) covers up the blunder to allow his name to live on in the army's history of heroism.

RED RIVER. United Artists 1948. Produced and directed by Howard Hawks. Cast: John Wayne, Montgomery Clift, Joanne Dru, Walter Brennan, Coleen Gray, John Ireland, Noah Berry Jr., Harry Carey, Harry Carey Jr., Paul Fix, Mickey Kuhn, Chief Yowlachie, Ivan Parry, Ray Hyke, Hank Worden, Dan White, Paul Fiero, William Self, Hal Taliaferro, Tom Tyler, Lane Chandler, Glenn Strange, Shelley Winters. Wayne, as Thomas Dunson, leads a cattle drive with his foster son (Clift) over the Chisolm Trail into Missouri. Wayne and Clift quarrel, split, and eventually reconcile after a fistfight.

THREE GODFATHERS. Metro-Goldwyn-Mayer 1949. Directed by John Ford. (Coproduced by Ford and Merian C. Cooper.) Cast: John Wayne, Pedro Armendariz, Harry Carey Jr., Ward Bond, Mae Marsh, Mildred Natwick, Jane Darwell, Guy Kibbee, Dorothy Ford, Ben Johnson, Charles Horton, Francis Ford. Wayne is Robert Marmaduke Sangster Hightower, one of three bank robbers who make their getaway across the desert, only to encounter an expectant mother inside a stalled covered wagon; they deliver the baby, but the mother dies and they stumble on to New Jerusalem, Arizona.

WAKE OF THE RED WITCH. Republic 1949. Directed by Edward Ludwig. Cast: John Wayne, Gail Russell, Gig Young, Adele Mara, Luther Adler, Eduard Franz, Grant Withers, Henry Daniell, Paul Fix, Dennis Hoey, Jeff Corey, Erskine Sanford, Duke Kahanamoku, Henry Brandon, Fernando Alvarado.

Wayne is sea captain of the *Red Witch*, which he deliberately sinks, and sails on another boat to a South Sea lagoon. (The *Red Witch* in the film is owned by a Dutch East Indies Trading Company, Batjak. Wayne later named his own film production company "Batjac.")

SHE WORE A YELLOW RIBBON. RKO Radio 1949. Directed by John Ford. (Coproduced by Ford and Merian C. Cooper.) Cast: John Wayne, Joanne Dru, John Agar, Ben Johnson, Harry Carey Jr., Victor McLaglen, Mildred Natwick, George O'Brien, Arthur Shields, Francis Ford, Harry Woods, Chief Big Tree, Noble Johnson, Cliff Lyons, Tom Tyler. Wayne is U. S. Cavalry Captain Nathan Brittles, on his last mission before retirement. (An Academy Award for photography; Monument Valley locations.)

THE FIGHTING KENTUCKIAN. Republic 1949. Directed and written by George Waggner. (Wayne's second film as producer.) Cast: John Wayne, Vera Ralston, Philip Dorn, Oliver Hardy, Marie Windsor, John Howard, Hugo Haas, Grant Withers, Mae Marsh, Paul Fix, Jack Pennick. Wayne plays a Daniel Boone-type Kentucky frontiersman in an 1820s story about a group of exiles from Napoleon's defeated armies.

SANDS OF IWO JIMA. Republic 1949. Directed by Allan Dwan. Cast: John Wayne, John Agar, Adele Mara, Forrest Tucker, Wally Cassell, James Brown, Richard Webb, Arthur Franz, Julie Bishop, James Holden, Peter Coe, Richard Jaeckel, Bill Murphy, George Tyne, Hal Fieberling (Hal Baylor), John McGuire, Martin Milner, Leonard Gumley, William Self, Dick Wessel, I. Stanford Jolley. Wayne as Sergeant John M. Stryker in the World War II story of Iwo Jima and the historic flag-raising on Mt. Suribachi. (Wayne's first nomination for a Best Actor Academy Award.)

RIO GRANDE. Republic 1950. Directed by John Ford. (Coproduced by Ford and Merian C. Cooper.) Cast: John Wayne, Maureen O'Hara, Ben Johnson, Claude Jarman Jr., Harry Carey Jr., J. Carrol Naish, Victor McLaglen, Grant Withers, Peter Ortiz, Steve Pendleton, Karolyn Grimes, Alberto Morin, Stan Jones, Fred Kennedy, Jack Pennick, Pat Wayne, Chuck Roberson. (Songs sung by The Sons of the Pioneers.) Wayne is Lieutenant Colonel Kirby Yorke in a story of a family, estranged since the Civil War fifteen years before, drawn together during the Apache wars near the Mexican border.

OPERATION PACIFIC. Warner Bros. 1951. Directed and written by George Waggner. Cast: John Wayne, Patricia Neal, Ward Bond, Scott Forbes, Philip Carey, Paul Picerni, Bill Campbell, Kathryn Givney, Martin Milner, Cliff Clark, Jack Pennick, Virginia Brissac, Vincent Forte, Lewis Martin. Wayne is Lieutenant Commander Duke Gifford aboard the submarine *Thunderfish*.

FLYING LEATHERNECKS. RKO Radio 1951. Directed by Nicholas Ray. Cast: John Wayne, Robert Ryan, Don Taylor, Janis Carter, Jay C. Flippen, William Harrigan, James Bell, Barry Kelley, Maurice Jara, Adam Williams, James Dobson, Carleton Young, Steve Flagg, Brett King, Gordon Gebert.

Wayne is Major Dan Kirby, head of a marine fighter squadron in the South Pacific.

THE QUIET MAN. Republic 1952. Directed by John Ford. Cast: John Wayne, Maureen O'Hara, Barry Fitzgerald, Ward Bond, Victor McLaglen, Mildred Natwick, Francis Ford, Eileen Crowe, May Craig, Arthur Shields, Charles FitzSimmons, James Lilburn, Sean McClory, Jack McGowran, Ken Curtis, Mae Marsh, Harry Tenbrook, Joseph O'Dea, Eric Gorman, Web Overlander, Patrick Wayne, Michael Wayne, Melinda Wayne, Antonia Wayne. (It won an Oscar for Ford and for its photography.) Wayne is Sean Thornton, a retired Irish-American boxer who returns to the land of his people.

BIG JIM McLAIN. Warner Bros. 1952. Directed by Edward Ludwig. Cast: John Wayne, Nancy Olson, James Arness, Alan Napier, Gayne Whitman, Hans Conreid, Veda Ann Borg, John Hubbard. Wayne is a special agent investigating a worldwide terror ring in Hawaii. (The first production under the banner of Wayne-Fellows, later Batjac.)

TROUBLE ALONG THE WAY. Warner Bros. 1953. Directed by Michael Curtiz. Cast: John Wayne, Donna Reed, Charles Coburn, Tom Tully, Marie Windsor, Sherry Jackson, Tom Helmore, Chuck Connors. Wayne is a former football player hired to coach a Catholic school team.

ISLAND IN THE SKY. Warner Bros. 1953. Directed by William A. Wellman. Cast: John Wayne, Lloyd Nolan, Walter Abel, James Arness, Andy Devine, Allyn Joslyn, James Lydon, Harry Carey Jr., Hal Baylor, Sean McClory, Sumner Getchell, Regis Toomey, Paul Fix, Bob Steele, Darryl Hickman. Wayne is one of a group of civilian pilots downed in Labrador.

HONDO. Warner Bros. 1953. Directed by John Farrow. Cast: John Wayne, Geraldine Page, Ward Bond, Michael Pate, Lee Aaker, James Arness, Rodolfo Acosta, Leo Gordon, Tom Irish, Paul Fix. Wayne is a dispatch rider for the U. S. Cavalry in the Southwest.

THE HIGH AND THE MIGHTY. Warner Bros. 1954. Directed by William A. Wellman. Cast: John Wayne, Claire Trevor, Laraine Day, Robert Stack, Jan Sterling, Phil Harris, Robert Newton, David Brian, Paul Kelly, Sidney Blackmer, Doe Avedon, Karen Sharpe, Pedro Gonzalez-Gonzalez, Paul Fix, John Qualen, Ann Doran. Trouble aboard a Honolulu-San Francisco airliner, with Wayne as copilot Dan Roman.

THE SEA CHASE. Warner Bros. 1955. Directed and produced by John Farrow. Cast: John Wayne, Lana Turner, David Farrar, Lyle Bettger, Tab Hunter, James Arness, Richard Davalos, John Qualen, Paul Fix, Alan Hale, Claude Akins. Wayne is captain of an outlaw freighter.

BLOOD ALLEY. Warner Bros. 1955. Directed by William A. Wellman. Cast: John Wayne, Lauren Bacall, Paul Fix, Joy Kim, Berry Kroeger, Mike Mazurki, Anita Ekberg, Henry Nakamura, W. T. Chang, George Chan. Wayne is a merchant marine

The Sons of Katie Elder; *John Wayne.*

captain who guides a ship through the dangerous Formosa Straits, "Blood Alley."

THE CONQUEROR. RKO Radio 1956. Directed and produced by Dick Powell. Cast: John Wayne, Susan Hayward, Pedro Armendariz, Agnes Moorehead, Thomas Gomez, John Hoyt, William Conrad, Ted de Corsia, Leslie Bradley, Leo Gordon, Lee Van Cleef, Peter Mamakos, Richard Loo. Wayne as a Mongol warrior who becomes Genghis Khan.

THE SEARCHERS. Warner Bros. 1956. Directed by John Ford. Cast: John Wayne, Jeffrey Hunter, Vera Miles, Natalie Wood, John Qualen, Olive Carey, Henry Brandon, Ken Curtis, Harry Carey Jr., Ward Bond, Antonio Moreno, Hank Worden, Lana Wood, Dorothy Jordan, Pippa Scott, Pat Wayne, Jack Pennick. The search for a little girl kidnapped by Comanches.

THE WINGS OF EAGLES. Metro-Goldwyn-Mayer 1957. Directed by John Ford. Cast: John Wayne, Dan Dailey, Maureen O'Hara, Ward Bond, Ken Curtis, Edmund Lowe, Kenneth Tobey, James Todd, Barry Kelley, Sig Ruman, Henry O'Neill, Willis Bouchey, Dorothy Jordan, Tige Andrews, Dan Borzage. Based on the life of navy aviation Commander Frank W. "Spig" Wead.

JET PILOT. RKO Radio 1957. Directed by Josef von Sternberg. Cast: John Wayne, Janet Leigh, Jay C. Flippen, Paul Fix, Richard Rober, Roland Winters, Hans Conried, Ivan Triesault, John Bishop, Perdita Chandler, Joyce Compton, Denver Pyle. Wayne is a U. S. jet pilot, Leigh a lieutenant in the Soviet air force who escapes from Russia.

LEGEND OF THE LOST. United Artists 1957. Directed and produced by Henry Hathaway. Cast: John Wayne, Sophia Loren, Rossano Brazzi, Kurt Kaszner, Sonia Moser. Wayne is a Sahara Desert guide.

I MARRIED A WOMAN. RKO Radio 1958. Directed by Hal Kanter. Cast: George Gobel, Diana Dors, Adolphe Menjou, Jessie Royce-Landis, Nita Talbot, William Redfield, Steven Dunne, John McGiver. John Wayne is in several scenes portraying beauty contest winner Diana Dors' favorite movie star.

THE BARBARIAN AND THE GEISHA. 20th Century-Fox 1958. Directed by John Huston. Cast: John Wayne, Eiko Ando, Sam Jaffe, So Yamamura, Norman Thomson, James Robbins, Morita, Kodaya Ichikawa. (Originally *The Townsend Harris Story*.) Biographical story of the first U. S. diplomatic representative to Japan in 1856.

RIO BRAVO. Warner Bros. 1959. Directed and produced by Howard Hawks. Cast: John Wayne, Dean Martin, Ricky Nelson, Angie Dickinson, Walter Brennan, Ward Bond, John Russell, Pedro Gonzalez-Gonzalez, Claude Akins, Malcolm Atterbury, Harry Carey Jr., Bob Steele, Myron Healey, Fred Graham, Riley Hill, Tom Monroe, Estelita Rodriguez. Wayne is Sheriff John T. Chance fighting a gang of gunmen after his prisoner.

THE HORSE SOLDIERS. United Artists 1959. Directed by John Ford. Cast: John Wayne, William Holden, Constance Towers, Althea Gibson, Hoot Gibson, Anna Lee, Russell Simpson, Stan Jones, Carleton Young, Basil Ruysdael, Willis Bouchey, Ken Curtis, O. Z. Whitehead, Judson Pratt, Denver Pyle, Strother Martin. Wayne is Colonel John Marlowe leading a U. S. Cavalry raid behind the Confederate lines in 1863.

THE ALAMO. United Artists 1960. Directed and produced by John Wayne. Cast: John Wayne, Richard Widmark, Laurence Harvey, Richard Boone, Frankie Avalon, Patrick Wayne, Linda Cristal, Joan O'Brien, Chill Wills, Joseph Calleia, Carlos Arruza, Ken Curtis, Hank Worden, Denver Pyle, Aissa Wayne, Julian Trevino, Jester Hairston, Veda Ann Borg, Olive Carey, Wesley Lau, Tom Hennessey, Bill Henry, Cy Malis, John Dierkes, Guinn Williams, Jack Pennick, Fred Graham, Bill Daniel, Chuck Roberson. Wayne is Davy Crockett in the historical story of the fight for Texas independence against the superior forces of Mexican army General Santa Anna.

NORTH TO ALASKA. 20th Century-Fox 1960. Directed and produced by Henry Hathaway. Cast: John Wayne, Stewart Granger, Ernie Kovacs, Fabian, Capucine, Mickey Shaughnessy, Karl Swenson, Joseph Sawyer, Kathleen Freeman, John Qualen, Stanley Adams, Stephen Courtleigh, Douglas Dick, Jerry O'Sullivan. Striking it rich in Alaska (actually Northern California).

THE COMANCHEROS. 20th Century-Fox 1961. Directed by Michael Curtiz. Cast: John Wayne, Stuart Whitman, Ina Balin, Nehemiah Persoff, Lee Marvin, Michael Ansara, Pat Wayne, Bruce Cabot, Joan O'Brien, Jack Elam, Edgar Buchanan, Henry Daniell, Bob Steele, Aissa Wayne. Wayne is a Texas Ranger captain against the Comancheros, an outlaw band supplying liquor and rifles to the Comanches.

THE MAN WHO SHOT LIBERTY VALANCE. Paramount 1962. Directed by John Ford. Cast: John Wayne, James Stewart, Vera Miles, Lee Marvin, Edmond O'Brien, Andy Devine, Woody Strode, John Qualen, Jeanette Nolan, Lee Van Cleef, Strother Martin, Ken Murray, John Carradine, Willis Bouchey. In flashback, a reporter hears the story of John Wayne/Tom Doniphon, the man who really shot gunman Liberty Valance, not Senator Ranse Stoddard/James Stewart, who became senator on that reputation. (And the famous line: "It ain't news. This is the West. When the legend becomes a fact, print the legend.")

HATARI! Paramount 1962. Directed and produced by Howard Hawks. Cast: John Wayne, Hardy Kruger, Elsa Martinelli, Red Buttons, Gérard Blain, Michèle Girardon, Bruce Cabot, Valentin De Vargas, Eduard Franz, Jon Chevron, Queenie Leonard. Wild game catching in East Africa.

THE LONGEST DAY. 20th Century-Fox 1963. Directed by Ken Annakin, Andrew Marton, Bernhard Wicki. Wayne is Lieutenant Colonel Benjamin Vandervoort in one of the episodes in the film story of D-Day by Cornelius Ryan.

HOW THE WEST WAS WON. Metro-Goldwyn-Mayer/

The Green Berets: *John Wayne.*

Cinerama 1962. Directed by Henry Hathaway, John Ford, George Marshall. John Wayne plays General William Tecumseh Sherman in a Civil War sequence, directed by Ford, in the film story of half a century of America's expansion.

DONOVAN'S REEF. Paramount 1963. Directed and produced by John Ford. Cast: John Wayne, Lee Marvin, Jack Warden, Elizabeth Allen, Cesar Romero, Dorothy Lamour, Jacqueline Malouf, Mike Mazurki, Edgar Buchanan, Pat Wayne, Chuck Roberson, Mae Marsh. Wayne is—note the name—Michael Patrick ''Guns'' Donovan, ex-navy man who, along with Lee Marvin, retired to a South Seas island.

McLINTOCK! United Artists 1963. Directed by Andrew V. McLaglen. (Produced by Michael Wayne.) Cast: John Wayne, Maureen O'Hara, Pat Wayne, Stefanie Powers, Yvonne De Carlo, Jack Kruschen, Chill Wills, Jerry Van Dyke, Edgar Buchanan, Bruce Cabot, Strother Martin, Aissa Wayne. Wayne having fun with Maureen O'Hara, the wife who left him, and Yvonne De Carlo, the widow he has hired as cook.

CIRCUS WORLD. Paramount 1964. Directed by Henry Hathaway. Cast: John Wayne, Claudia Cardinale, Rita Hayworth, Lloyd Nolan, Richard Conte, John Smith, Henri Dantes, Wanda Rotha, Kay Walsh, Katharyna. American impresario Wayne takes his Wild West show to Europe.

THE GREATEST STORY EVER TOLD. United Artists 1965. Directed and produced by George Stevens. John Wayne plays a Roman centurion who leads Jesus to the crucifixion in this biblical story of the life of Jesus.

IN HARM'S WAY. Paramount 1965. Directed and produced by Otto Preminger. Cast: John Wayne, Kirk Douglas, Patricia Neal, Tom Tryon, Paula Prentiss, Brandon De Wilde, Jill Haworth, Dana Andrews, Stanley Holloway, Burgess Meredith, Franchot Tone, Patrick O'Neal, Carroll O'Connor, Slim Pickens, James Mitchum, Barbara Bouchet, Hugh O'Brian, Henry Fonda, George Kennedy, Tod Andrews, Larry Hagman, Soo Yong. Wayne is Captain Rockwell Torrey, commander of a cruiser in Pearl Harbor on December 7, 1941.

THE SONS OF KATIE ELDER. Paramount 1965. Directed by Henry Hathaway. Cast: John Wayne, Dean Martin, Martha Hyer, Michael Anderson Jr., Earl Holliman, Jeremy Slate, James Gregory, Paul Fix, George Kennedy, Dennis Hopper, John Litel, Strother Martin, Rhys Williams, John Qualen, Percy Kelton. Wayne is the oldest of four sons who regain respectability for the Elder name.

CAST A GIANT SHADOW. United Artists 1966. Directed, produced, and written by Melville Shavelson. (Coproduced by Michael Wayne.) Cast: Kirk Douglas, Yul Brynner, Senta Berger, Angie Dickinson, Luther Adler, Stathis Giallelis, James Donald, Gordon Jackson, Chaim Topol, Frank Sinatra, John Wayne, Ruth White. Wayne is an American general in the story of Israeli-American Colonel David Marcus.

THE WAR WAGON. Universal 1967. Directed by Burt Ken-

Rio Lobo: *John Wayne.*

True Grit: *John Wayne.*

nedy. Cast: John Wayne, Kirk Douglas, Howard Keel, Robert Walker, Keenan Wynn, Bruce Cabot, Valora Noland, Gene Evans, Joanna Barnes. Wayne, out of prison, plans vengeance on the man who defrauded him.

EL DORADO. Paramount 1967. Directed and produced by Howard Hawks. Cast: John Wayne, Robert Mitchum, James Caan, Charlene Holt, Michele Carey, Arthur Hunnicutt, R. G. Armstrong, Edward Asner, Paul Fix, Johnny Crawford, Western brawling starting in the Broken Heart Saloon at El Dorado.

THE GREEN BERETS. Warner Bros./Seven Arts 1968. Directed by John Wayne and Ray Kellogg; produced by Michael Wayne. Cast: John Wayne, David Janssen, Jim Hutton, Aldo Ray, Raymond St. Jacques, Bruce Cabot, Jack Soo, George Takei, Pat Wayne, Irene Tsu, Edward Faulkner, Jason Evers, Mike Henry. U. S. Special Forces, known as the Green Berets, in Vietnam.

HELLFIGHTERS. Universal 1969. Directed by Andrew V. McLaglen. Cast: John Wayne, Katharine Ross, Vera Miles, Jim Hutton, Jay C. Flippen, Bruce Cabot, Edward Faulkner, Barbara Stuart. A story of oil firefighters.

TRUE GRIT. Paramount 1969. Directed by Henry Hathaway. Cast: John Wayne, Glen Campbell, Kim Darby, Jeremy Slate, Robert Duvall, Dennis Hopper, Alfred Ryder, Strother Martin, Jeff Corey, Ron Soble, John Fielder. Wayne is rough, tough, hard-drinking U. S. Marshal Rooster Cogburn, who helps Kim Darby track down her father's killer. Wayne's Best Actor Academy Award.

THE UNDEFEATED. 20th Century-Fox 1969. Directed by Andrew V. McLaglen. Cast: John Wayne, Rock Hudson, Antonio Aguilar, Roman Gabriel, Marian McCargo, Lee Meriwether, Merlin Olsen, Melissa Newman, Bruce Cabot, Ben Johnson, Paul Fix, Harry Carey Jr., Royal Dano, John Agar, Pedro Armendariz Jr. Wayne is a U. S. Cavalry officer who gets involved with Emperor Maximilian's troubles in Mexico after the Civil War.

CHISUM. Warner Bros. 1970. Directed by Andrew V.

The Cowboys: *John Wayne.*

McQ: *John Wayne.*

Cahill, U.S. Marshal: *John Wayne.*

McLaglen. Cast: John Wayne, Forrest Tucker, Christopher George, Ben Johnson, Glenn Corbett, Andrew Prine, Bruce Cabot, Richard Jaeckel, Lynda Day, John Agar, Edward Faulkner, Pedro Armendariz Jr., Christopher Mitchum. Wayne is wealthy landowner John Simpson Chisum in a bloody cattle war in New Mexico Territory in the late 1800s.

RIO LOBO. Cinema Center 1970. Directed by Howard Hawks. Cast: John Wayne, Jennifer O'Neill, Jack Elam, Jorge Rivero, Christopher Mitchum, Dave Huddleston, Peter Jason. Wayne is an ex-Civil War officer who helps free a Texas town of carpetbaggers.

BIG JAKE. National General 1971. Directed by George Sherman. (Produced by Michael Wayne.) Cast: John Wayne, Richard Boone, Maureen O'Hara, Patrick Wayne, Christopher Mitchum, Bobby Vinton, Bruce Cabot, John Ethan Wayne. Wayne rescues kidnapped grandson.

THE COWBOYS. Warner Bros. 1972. Directed by Mark Rydell. Cast: John Wayne, Colleen Dewhurst, Slim Pickens, Roscoe

Lee Browne. Wayne is an old cattleman who recruits a bunch of schoolboys to help him as he teaches them the ways of the Old West.

THE TRAIN ROBBERS. Warner Bros. 1973. Directed and written by Burt Kennedy. (Produced by Michael Wayne.) Cast: John Wayne, Ann-Margret, Rod Taylor, Ben Johnson, Christopher George, Bobby Vinton, Jerry Gatlin, Ricardo Montalban. Wayne helps the widow get her rightful share of the gold.

CAHILL, U. S. MARSHAL. Warner Bros. 1973. Directed by Andrew V. McLaglen. (Produced by Michael Wayne.) Cast: John Wayne, Gary Grimes, Neville Brand, Clay O'Brien, Marie Windsor, Morgan Paull, Dan Vadis, Royal Dano, Scott Walker, Denver Pyle, Jackie Coogan, Harry Carey Jr., Paul Fix, George Kennedy. Wayne is the marshal whose two sons get mixed up with bank robbers and murder.

McQ. Warner Bros. 1974. Directed by John Sturges. Cast: John Wayne, Eddie Albert, Diana Muldaur, Colleen Dewhurst, Clu Gulager, David Huddleston, Jim Watkins, Al Lettieri. Wayne is a city detective who quits the force to revenge his buddy's murder.

BRANNIGAN. United Artists 1975. Directed by Douglas Hickox. Cast: John Wayne, Richard Attenborough, Judy Geeson, Mel Ferrer, John Vernon, Daniel Pilon, John Stride, James Booth, Del Henney, Lesley Ann Down, Barry Dennen, Anthony Booth, Brian Glover, Ralph Meeker, Jack Watson. Wayne plays an Irish cop from Chicago who goes to London to get his man.

ROOSTER COGBURN. Universal 1975. Directed by Stuart Millar. Cast: John Wayne, Katharine Hepburn, Anthony Zerbe, Strother Martin, Richard Jordan, John McIntire, Paul Koslo, Jon Lormer, Richard Romancito. Rooster Cogburn again, this time helping find the murderers of a spinster's minister father, as well as stolen nitro.

THE SHOOTIST. Paramount 1976. Directed by Don Siegel. Cast: John Wayne, Lauren Bacall, Ron Howard, James Stewart, Richard Boone, John Carradine, Scatman Crothers, Richard Lenz, Harry Morgan, Sheree North, Hugh O'Brian. Wayne as J. B. Books, aging gunman dying of cancer, gets killed in a barroom shootout—choosing to die ''with his boots on.''